A VISUAL APPROACH TO ALGEBRA

D1368652

Frances Van Dyke

DALE SEYMOUR PUBLICATIONS®
WHITE PLAINS, NEW YORK

ACKNOWLEDGMENTS

I wish to thank all the people who directly or indirectly helped me with this book. Those people are:

- For perceptive comments and suggestions on many articles, Tim Craine.
- For editorial assistance, Carol Zacny and Nancy R. Anderson.
- For an outstanding two-year Math Technology Institute, Bob Decker, Leslie Paoletti, Kathy Watson.
- For collaborative work on calculus and algebra courses, Charlie Waiveris.
- For encouragement and support during several academic years, Bill Driscoll.
- For flexibility, patience, and help with chaos, Pat Kelly.
- For their love and support, my husband Ted and my children Chris, Hugo, and Mary. This book is dedicated to them and to the memory of two other Hugos and two Nancys.

Senior Mathematics Editor: Carol Zacny

Project Editor: Nancy R. Anderson

Production Coordinator: Joe Conte

Design Manager: Jeff Kelly

Cover design: Don Taka

Text design: Don Taka

Electronic prepress: A. W. Kingston Publishing Services, Chandler, AZ

This book is published by Dale Seymour Publications®, an imprint of Addison Wesley Longman, Inc.

Dale Seymour Publications
10 Bank Street
White Plains, NY 10602
Customer Service: 800-872-1100

Order number DS21838

ISBN 1-57232-441-4

2 3 4 5 6 7 8 9 10-ML-03 02 01 00 99 98

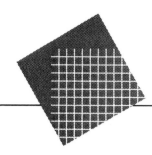

TABLE OF CONTENTS

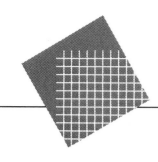

INTRODUCTION: A VISUAL APPROACH TO ALGEBRA

This book is designed to be a resource for both middle- and high-school teachers. The idea for the book grew out of my attempt to teach a college-algebra course in the spirit of the calculus-reform movement and the NCTM Standards. The reform movement urges us to emphasize concepts and ideas rather than processes, and to present each topic algebraically, visually, and numerically. The notion of a function is central to the college-algebra course and lends itself nicely to these three modes of presentation. In my college-algebra class, however, students were wedded to the algebraic representation and very reluctant to use any other form.

In looking through high-school texts, I found there was a very heavy emphasis on algebraic processes and little or no attempt to develop concepts visually or give exercises with a visual component. Consequently, I wrote for *The Mathematics Teacher*, September 1994, an article in which I gave ideas for visual exercises. After finishing the article, I felt that teachers really needed many more exercises in order to implement the ideas presented in the article. I also began to think of other ways in which visual exercises could be used to enhance learning and to help students overcome certain misconceptions. It seemed to me appropriate to write a resource book in which all the exercises had a visual component.

There are a variety of reasons for the curriculum to become more visual in the upper grades. Developmentally, the capacity to think in images precedes the capacity to think in words. Understanding follows the same pattern. Elementary-school texts have taken full advantage of visual images but high-school texts do not continue in that mode. Students of this generation are far more sophisticated visually than were students of preceding generations. We need to take advantage of this sophistication and use it to help students understand mathematical concepts and strengthen their connection with mathematics. Students whose first language is not English are at less of a disadvantage if the material is presented visually as well as verbally. A visual approach may, in particular, help students who do not consider themselves mathematically oriented.

The recent addition of graphing calculators to the classroom has underscored the need for more and different types of graphing exercises at an earlier age. The majority of students in their first algebra course initially have a very difficult time writing the correct algebraic equation that corresponds to a given verbal statement. Picturing the correct graph when given a statement is an easier process, and intermediate exercises of this type can get middle-school students to begin thinking abstractly. Some students will understand a relationship more fully if it is pictured; for these students, the graph needs to be there from the beginning.

Traditionally, students have a hard time associating what they do in the mathematics classroom with their daily lives and the world around them. A sense that mathematics is ever present in our lives and can be used to describe and simplify relations between quantities encountered every day may inspire students who formerly were easily turned off from mathematics.

This book is divided into lessons that consist of notes for the teacher, giving answers and background material, and a blackline master of the student worksheet. The teacher notes for the first lesson are given in much greater detail than are the notes for the following lessons. They are intended to model the questioning procedure that should be used with all lessons.

Typically, the exercises can be done by students working collaboratively in groups or by individuals. In general, however, not every lesson need be covered. This is a resource book designed to supplement standard texts. You should not feel obligated to start at the beginning and proceed through to the end. Rather, look for topics that may intrigue your students and or help them solidify their understanding of important material.

Lessons in Chapter 1 are designed to help students realize that a graph is a legitimate representation of a relationship, to encourage them to begin thinking on an abstract level, and to help them connect mathematics with situations encountered in everyday life. These objectives are appropriate for all math students from grade 7 on. The graphs in Chapter 1 are qualitative and do not include scales. The exercises consist of identifying, drawing, and interpreting graphs. The notion of increasing and decreasing rates of change is of utmost importance in calculus and often gives students trouble. In Lessons 1.6 and 1.7 of Chapter 1, rates of change are introduced on a simple level. You are urged to try these lessons with your classes.

Once they have been introduced to visualizing relationships, students can start to get a sense of different types of growth. In some applications, the growth is linear; in others, it is exponential. At this point, the students do not need to know which type of growth to expect; but they will learn to associate the correct type with the specific application, as it will be the only viable option. In Chapter 2, the notion of scale is introduced. Many of the graphs in this chapter look at distance as a function of time. These lessons are appropriate for high-school students beginning a course in algebra.

Students can explore a formula visually by doing graphing exercises in which all but two variables in the formula are held constant and the resulting relationship is pictured. This type of exercise is covered in Chapter 3. Before collecting data in an experiment, students can complete visual exercises to help familiarize themselves with the language of the experiment and to get them to think about possible results. The lessons in Chapter 3 should be done by students who have an interest in the formulas and experiments contained in the lessons.

Chapter 4 begins with exercises on the Pythagorean theorem and then visually explores several concepts from the standard algebra curriculum. These include distance between points, slope of a line, and slopes of parallel and perpendicular lines. In algebra classes, students often fail to see that a graph and the corresponding algebraic equation are two representations for the same set of points. The two representations have such different appearances that the intimate connection between them is lost. Students also have a difficult time representing a relationship between quantities with an appropriate equation.

There are several lessons in Chapter 4 designed to help students recognize the correct equation for a verbal statement. Even when students can derive a correct algebraic equation from a statement and graph that equation, they often have difficulty in then taking an arbitrary point on the graph that lies within the natural domain of the function and using it to make an appropriate statement in terms of the original verbal problem. The lessons in this chapter will intimately link the equation with the graph by pointing out that questions about the verbal situation can be answered using either representation. As understanding linear functions should be a major goal of a first course in algebra, the treatment of linear functions in this chapter is very thorough.

A glossary is included in the back of this book. The Glossary gives informal definitions of some of the more difficult or confusing terms and vocabulary.

CHAPTER 1   PICTURING RELATIONSHIPS

We use mathematics to understand relationships between quantities. Mathematical models can be employed to help us make predictions as well as comprehend relationships. In this chapter, we look at, interpret, and draw a variety of graphs. The exercises are designed to help students:

- interpret graphs
- think on an abstract level
- connect mathematics with the world around them
- understand the notion of a function
- learn to expect a particular shape for the graphs of certain functions
- enjoy their math class

The material in Chapter 1 is appropriate for middle- or high-school students. However, if the students have had algebra, they may be able to supply algebraic representations for the graphs shown. These are referred to in the teacher notes and may be ignored if the material is being used in a course preceding algebra.

In the first eleven lessons of this chapter, students must choose from four choices the graph that best matches a verbal statement. Many of these examples refer to relationships between quantities that will be studied in detail in the students' high-school math classes. Population growth, exponential decay, and distance as a function of time are all standard topics in advanced algebra. We want the students to become very familiar with these functions and to develop a sense of what type of graph to expect when these functions are studied. In order for students to develop this familiarity, it is suggested that you read each exercise aloud for the first few lessons and ensure that every student has a clear mental image of the situation presented in the verbal statement. As an example, consider the first exercise of Lesson 1.1. The statement indicates that a hot piece of aluminum foil cools to the temperature of the room. When asked what happens to the temperature of the foil as time passes, someone may answer using the words of the problem, saying that the foil cools. You could then ask these questions:

- Does the temperature of the foil fall or rise as time passes?
- Does the temperature increase or decrease?
- Does the temperature go up or go down?

We want every student to fully understand that as time goes by, the temperature of the foil drops. Ask students:

- What do you think is the classroom temperature?
- What temperatures are the rooms in your houses?
- What do you consider to be a good temperature for a room?

  Have you ever been in a room in which the temperature was zero?

  After the first few lessons, such detailed questioning may not be necessary.

In Lessons 1.12–1.16, there are exercises in which a situation is described and students must interpret a given graph or graph a relationship inherent to the situation. There are also exercises in which students must create their own examples or study a graph and describe a relationship the graph could model.

TEACHER NOTES

Exercises 1 and 2

A hot piece of aluminum foil cools and we graph the temperature of the foil as a function of time. In the future, students will learn that such a relationship can be modeled by an exponential function. Here, we want them to think only about what happens to the temperature of the foil as time passes and to choose the graph which best illustrates this.

As stated in the introduction, you should make sure everyone fully understands the situation. Discuss each choice before having the students choose the answer, or at least refrain from commenting on student answers until each choice has been considered.

To help students understand what is being measured along each axis, ask:

- What is measured along the horizontal axis? *(Time elapsed)*
- What happens as we move farther and farther to the right? *(More and more time goes by.)*
- What is measured along the vertical axis? *(Temperature of the foil)*
- What happens as we move higher and higher on the vertical axis? *(The points correspond to hotter and hotter initial temperatures.)*
- Finally, for each graph, ask students what happens to the temperature as time goes by. In graph **a**, the temperature remains the same. *(For algebra students only:* An algebraic description for this graph is $T(x)$ = any positive number. If the graph describes a steady room temperature, the number is that temperature.) In graph **b**, the temperature decreases steadily until it reaches zero. *(For algebra students only:* An algebraic description for this graph is $T(x) = mx + b$. As no scale is indicated, in terms of the graph any choice of m and b is acceptable provided m is negative and b is positive.) In both graphs **a** and **b**, temperature is a *function* of time, as for any particular time there is exactly one temperature. In graph **c**, the temperature remains constant for a short time and then drops suddenly. This pattern is repeated several times. The vertical lines in this graph indicate a range of temperatures for a particular time. This graph does not describe the situation and is indeed not the graph of a function. In graph **d**, the temperature decreases rapidly at first and then more and more slowly as the temperature of the foil gets closer and closer to room temperature. Have students note that graph **d** is also the graph of a function.

1. Graph **d**; if students suggest graph **b**, explain that substances cool naturally in this manner rather than at a steady rate.
2. Students' paragraphs should explain what happens to the temperature in each graph as time passes, as described above.

Note: This experiment can be done with a hair dryer and foil if the school has a TI-82 overhead and a CBL unit (a hand-held calculator-based laboratory for data collection). See Lesson 3.6.

Exercises 3 and 4

These exercises involve a boy who raises a book above his head and then drops
the book. The distance of the book from the floor is graphed as a function of time.
In the future, students will learn that such a relationship can be modeled by a
quadratic function. Here, we want them to think only about how the height of the
book above the floor changes with time and to identify the graph which best
pictures this. The pitfall for students is that they may choose graph **b**, but this
graph shows no passage of time as the book falls.

Ask:

■ What happens to the height of the book above the ground as time passes. *(The
height first increases and then decreases.)*

■ Once the fall has started, will the height keep changing until the book reaches
the floor? *(Yes)*

■ At a particular point in time is there more than one height for the book? *(No)*
The fact that for any one given time there is a unique height tells us that height
is a function of time.

Again, to help students understand what is being measured along each axis, ask:

■ What is measured along the horizontal axis? *(Time elapsed)*

■ What happens as we move farther and farther to the right? *(More and more
time goes by.)*

■ What is measured along the vertical axis? *(Distance of the book from the floor)*

■ What happens as we move higher and higher on the vertical axis? *(The points
correspond to greater and greater original heights for the book.)*

Next ask the students to consider what is happening in each graph. In graph **a**,
the height increases and decreases twice, indicating that the book was raised,
lowered, raised again, and then dropped. In graph **b**, the book is raised and held
and then there is a vertical line, indicating that no time passes as the book falls. In
graph **c**, the height slightly increases as the person raises the book and then
decreases as the book is dropped. In graph **d**, the height slightly increases and then
decreases, but it decreases at a slower and slower rate. You could point out that
while the decrease does match the way a hot substance cools, it does not correspond
to the way things drop. Additionally, the book never reaches the ground.

3. Graph **c**
4. Students' paragraphs should include the descriptions above and their
   explanations of their choice of graph.

You may want to assess students' work by grading their answers to Exercises **2**
and **4**.

Extension

As an extension to this lesson, you might have students perform one or more of the following:

A Drop objects and record data using a CBL unit and a motion detector. (See Lesson 3.7.)

B Draw a graph that might model the temperature of a cup of hot tea as it cools to room temperature, with temperature as a function of time.

C Draw a graph that might model the height of a dropped balloon as a function of time.

D If a CBL is available, the experiments in B and C can be done using the unit. In any case, the two graphs should be compared and their shapes contrasted.

For each set of graphs, choose the one that best matches the situation.

1. A hot piece of aluminum foil cools to the temperature of the room.

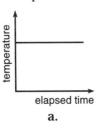

a.

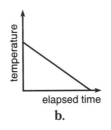

b.

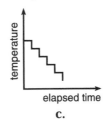

c.

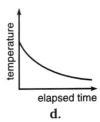

d.

2. After discussing the graphs of Exercise **1** with classmates, write a short paragraph explaining what is happening in each of the graphs.

3. A boy raises a book above his head and then lets the book fall.

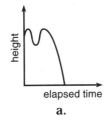

a.

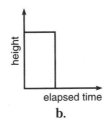

b.

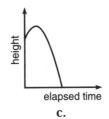

c.

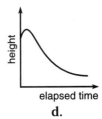

d.

4. After discussing the graphs of Exercise **3** with classmates, write a short paragraph justifying your answer. How does your choice describe the motion? Why are the other graphs inappropriate?

TEACHER NOTES

This exercise set is appropriate for beginning algebra students. The follow-up activities should be done by students who have studied linear functions.

Exercise 1

Graph **a**; most students will know how many miles per gallon their family car gets, and the amount of gas in the tank can be seen as a decreasing linear function with the magnitude of the slope as the reciprocal of that number. If the tank is full and holds 18 gallons and the car gets 28 miles to the gallon, an approximation to the amount of gas in the tank x miles from the station where you filled up would be $y = 18 - \frac{1}{28}x$. Some students may argue that the car uses more gas in town than on the highway, so graph **d** is a possibility as well. Since we were not told the car first was in local traffic and then on the highway, graph **a** seems the better choice. Graphs **b** and **c** are clearly not correct as the amount of gas in the tank does not increase as distance is traveled.

Exercise 2

Graph **a**; here there is no ambiguity, as $A = s^2$. Graph **b** is clearly incorrect, as area can never decrease when side length increases. Graph **c** is also incorrect as area cannot remain constant as side length increases. One can plot points or look at numerical differences to see that graph **a**, not graph **d**, is the correct shape for this increasing function.

Exercise 3

Graph **b**; if one gram of fudge contains 90 calories, a person consumes $90x$ calories while eating x grams. The graph of $y = 90x$ is a straight line that rises to the right. Students should be able to explain why the rest of the answers are inappropriate, as the graphs rise and fall or remain constant.

Exercise 4

Graph **a**; the formula for the perimeter of a square is $P = 4s$, and the graph is a straight line that rises to the right. Again, the rest of the choices are inappropriate, as the graphs rise and fall or remain constant.

Extension

As an extension to this lesson, you might have students perform the following:

A Find out the size of their family's car gas tank and how many miles to the gallon the car gets. Have them give the function that approximates the number of gallons in their tank *x* miles after fill-up. The class can compare functions and decide which car can go farthest between fill-ups. They should see that algebraically this is the function that has the greatest *x*-intercept.

B Make a table to see the effect on the perimeter and area of a square as side length increases from 1 unit to 10 units. Are the perimeter and the area the same for any side length? (Yes, when the length is 4; if the side length is less than 4, the perimeter is greater than the area. Students should note, however, that the perimeter is measured in units and the area in square units.) If the **a** graphs in Exercises 2 and 4 were graphed on the same set of axes, they would intersect at (4, 16). For side lengths less than 4, the graph of perimeter would be above the graph of area.

C Choose a food, find how many calories are in each gram of the food, and give the equation and graph for that food, with calories consumed as a function of grams eaten.

For each set of graphs, choose the graph that best matches the situation. Write a sentence explaining why you chose the particular graph you did.

1. The farther the car goes, the more gas it uses.

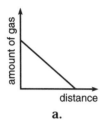
a.

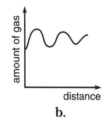
b.

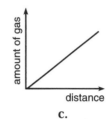
c.

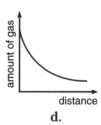
d.

2. As the length of the side of a square increases, its area increases.

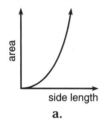
a.

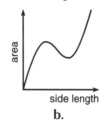
b.

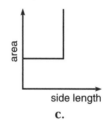
c.

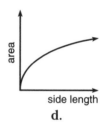
d.

3. The greater the number of grams of fudge eaten, the more calories consumed.

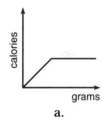
a.

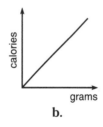
b.

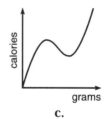
c.

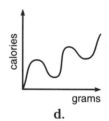
d.

4. As the length of the side of a square increases, its perimeter increases.

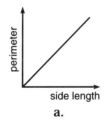
a.

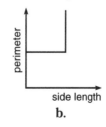
b.

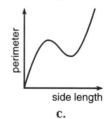
c.

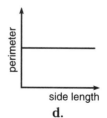
d.

TEACHER NOTES

The exercises here are straightforward and can be done at any level. Recommendations are given for students who have studied linear functions. This is a good lesson to do if the class is going to work with a motion detector and CBL unit. It will help students to think about how to create certain graphs when using the motion detector.

Exercise 1

Graph **a**; as time passes, the distance from the car increases. If they have studied linear functions, students should be able to state that this line will have an equation of the form $y = mx$ where m is positive.

Exercise 2

Graph **b**; as time passes, the distance from the car decreases. If they have studied linear functions, students should be able to state that this line will have an equation of the form $y = mx + b$ where m is negative and b is positive.

Exercise 3

Graph **c**; as time passes, the distance from the car does not change. If they have studied linear functions, students should be able to state that this line will have an equation of the form $y = c$, where c is a constant.

Exercise 4

Graph **c**; as time passes, the distance from the car decreases and then increases. (*For Algebra students only:* If they have studied linear functions and piecewise defined functions, students should be able to state the form of the algebraic expression which is:

$$f(x) = \begin{cases} mx+b, & x \leq c \\ kx+1, & x > c \end{cases}$$

In this equation, c represents the moment Nancy changes direction, and $m < 0$, $1 < 0$, $k > 0$, $b > 0$.)

For each set of graphs, choose one that best matches the situation. Write a sentence explaining why you chose the particular graph you did.

1. Hugo walked at a steady pace away from the car.

a.

b.

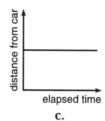

c.

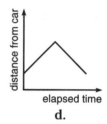

d.

2. Mary walked at a steady pace toward the car.

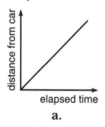

a.

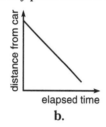

b.

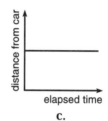

c.

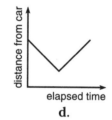

d.

3. Chris stood at a distance from the car.

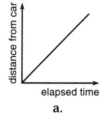

a.

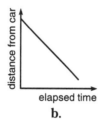

b.

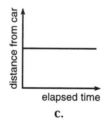

c.

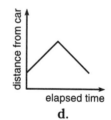

d.

4. Nancy first walked toward the car and then away from it.

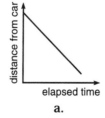

a.

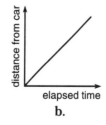

b.

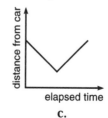

c.

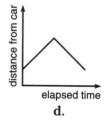

d.

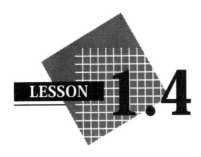

TEACHER NOTES

With this set of exercises, students can increase their proficiency in identifying the proper overall shape a graph must have, given a particular situation.

Exercise 1

Graph **c**; it is clear that neither graph **b** nor graph **d** is correct, as in graph **b** the temperature is rising and in graph **d** the temperature increases and decreases as time passes. Graph **a** can be eliminated, as substances do not cool at a constant rate. Students should recall this from earlier lessons.

Exercise 2

Graph **c**; it is the only graph in which the population increases as time passes. As this graph suggests, populations often increase in an exponential fashion.

Exercise 3

Graph **d**; it is the ony graph that conveys the idea that attention span will be low if the temperature is either very high or very low.

Exercise 4

Graph **a**; it is the only graph that shows that over time, the population first increases and then decreases.

For each set of graphs, choose the one that best matches the situation. Write a sentence explaining your choice.

1. After death, a body cools to the temperature of the room.

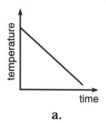 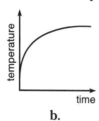 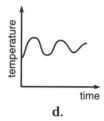 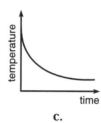

    a.   b.   c.   d.

2. The population has been increasing over the years.

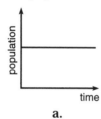 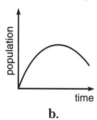 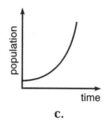 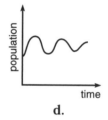

    a.   b.   c.   d.

3. The ideal temperature for a classroom is around 70° F. When the temperature rises above 70°F, the average student's attention span decreases. Similarly, if the temperature falls below 70°F, the attention span again will decrease.

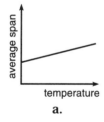 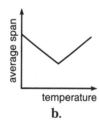 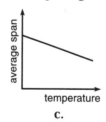 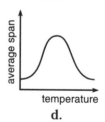

    a.   b.   c.   d.

4. In the 1930s in Arizona, the deer population first increased and then decreased until deer became extinct.

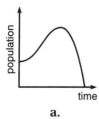 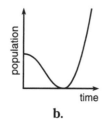 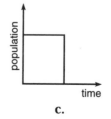 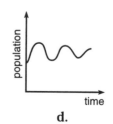

    a.   b.   c.   d.

TEACHER NOTES

This lesson will be helpful for students who are working with the formula, *distance* = *rate* × *time*. For the remainder of this page, *d* refers to distance, *t* to time, and *r* to rate. Once again, the lesson can be done at all levels and the references to the formula ignored.

Exercise 1

Graph **a**; students should be aware that speed, not distance, is graphed along the vertical axis. Some students may choose graph **d**, as speed is often depicted with a similar graph. For each graph, students should be able to describe the corresponding situation, recognizing that graph **a** is the only one that matches the statement.

Exercise 2

Graph **c**; here, the distance is held fixed and we are considering the relation $t = \frac{C}{r}$, where C is the constant corresponding to the mileage between New Haven and Boston.

Exercise 3

Graph **b**; as people often associate speed with increase, some students may choose graph **a**. You could ask for the algebraic description of the correct response, eliciting $y = C$, where C corresponds to the constant speed of the car.

Exercise 4

Graph **a**; here the time is held fixed and we are considering the relationship between distance and rate.

For each set of graphs, choose one that best matches the situation. Write a sentence explaining why you chose the particular graph you did.

1. Fumihiko kept increasing his speed until his mother made him slow down and proceed at a constant speed under the limit.

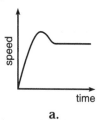

a.

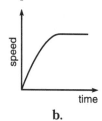

b.

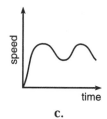

c.

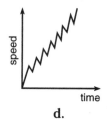

d.

2. On the trip from New Haven to Boston, the faster you go the less time it takes. Realize that as the speed increases the time required for the trip decreases.

a.

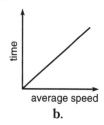

b.

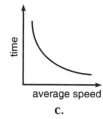

c.

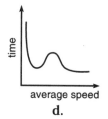

d.

3. Leila drove at a constant speed.

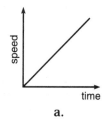

a.

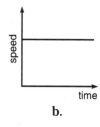

b.

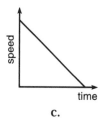

c.

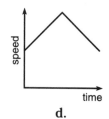

d.

4. The faster you go, the farther you go during any given time period.

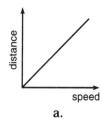

a.

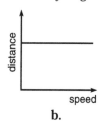

b.

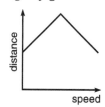

c.

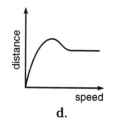

d.

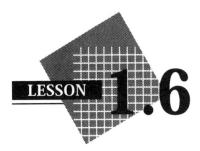

TEACHER NOTES

Lessons 1.6 and 1.7 introduce students to the idea of increasing and decreasing rates of change. This concept is very important in the study of calculus. Students may understand the idea most easily by considering the situation in Exercise 4 of Lesson 1.6, where a driver speeds up, slows down, or travels at a constant rate. Exercises 1–3 in Lesson 1.6 carefully examine the idea with examples of population growth. In Lesson 1.7, the idea is examined with examples of population decline.

Exercise 1

Graph **a** shows Fenterville's population as a function of time. As we move to the right by equal amounts along the horizontal axis, the corresponding increases in population become smaller and smaller. Fenterville's population growth is slowing down. If this trend of a decreasing growth rate continues, the rate may become zero and then negative, indicating that the town's population is decreasing.

Exercise 2

Graph **b** shows Denterville's population as a function of time. As we move to the right by equal amounts along the horizontal axis, the corresponding increases in population become greater and greater.

Exercise 3

Graph **c** shows Centerville's population as a function of time. As we move to the right by equal amounts along the horizontal axis, the corresponding increases in population are also equal.

Exercise 4

In graph **a**, the speed is constant. For each unit of time, the driver covers the same distance. In graph **b**, the driver is slowing down. As time passes, the driver covers less distance in each unit of time. In graph **c**, the driver is speeding up. As time passes, the driver covers a greater distance in each unit of time.

The populations of Centerville, Denterville, and Fenterville are increasing. In each town at the end of every year, there are more people than there were at the beginning of the year.

■ In Centerville, the population is increasing at a constant rate. Every year, the population increases by the same amount.

■ In Denterville, the *rate* of increase is increasing. Every year, more and more people are moving to Denterville.

■ In Fenterville, the rate of increase is decreasing. Every year, the population is increasing by a smaller and smaller amount.

Below are three graphs, each of which shows population increasing as a function of time.

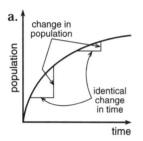

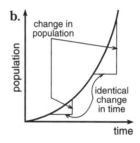

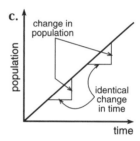

To help you decide which graph corresponds to each city, the graphs indicate two equal changes in time and the corresponding changes in population. In each case, time is passing as you move to the right along the horizontal axis. Compare the two changes in population that correspond to the two equal units of elapsed time.

1. Look carefully at graph **a**. Describe what you notice and determine which city's growth is shown.

2. Look carefully at graph **b**. Describe what you notice and determine which city's growth is shown.

3. Look carefully at graph **c**. Describe what you notice and determine which city's growth is shown.

4. If you are graphing distance traveled as a function of time, the rate of change represents speed. In one of the graphs below the speed is constant, in one the driver is speeding up, and in the third the driver is slowing down. Decide which graph pictures each situation. Write a sentence explaining your choice.

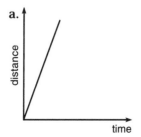

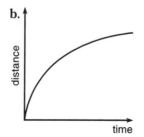

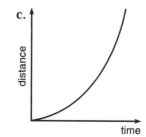

TEACHER NOTES

Exercise 1

Graph **a** shows Henterville's population as a function of time. As you move to the right by equal amounts along the horizontal axis, the corresponding decreases in population are also equal.

Exercise 2

Graph **b** shows Lenterville's population as a function of time. As you move to the right by equal amounts along the horizontal axis, the corresponding decreases in population are more pronounced. The decline in Lenterville's population is becoming more and more severe.

Exercise 3

Graph **c** shows Kenterville's population as a function of time. As you move to the right by equal amounts along the horizontal axis, the corresponding decreases in population are less pronounced.

Exercise 4

Graph **c**, because the rate of change in Kenterville is increasing as the population decreases; there is a smaller and smaller decline in population.

Exercise 5

Graph **b**, because the rate of change in Lenterville is decreasing as the population decreases; there is a greater and greater decline in population.

The populations of Henterville, Kenterville, and Lenterville are decreasing. In each town at the end of every year, there are fewer people than there were at the beginning of the year.

■ In Henterville, the population is decreasing at a constant rate. Every year, the population decreases by the same amount.

■ In Kenterville, the rate of change is increasing. Every year, although the population continues to decrease, fewer and fewer people leave.

■ In Lenterville, the rate of change is decreasing. Every year, the population is decreasing by a greater and greater amount.

Below are three graphs, each of which shows population decreasing as a function of time.

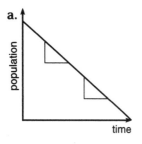 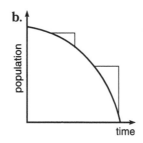 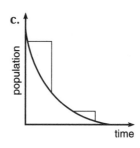

To help you decide which graph corresponds to each city, the graphs indicate two equal changes in time and the corresponding changes in population. In each case, time is passing as you move to the right along the horizontal axis. Compare the two changes in population that correspond to the two equal units of elapsed time.

1. Look carefully at graph **a**. Describe what you notice and determine which city's growth is shown.

2. Look carefully at graph **b**. Describe what you notice and determine which city's growth is shown.

3. Look carefully at graph **c**. Describe what you notice and determine which city's growth is shown.

4. Which graph shows a population that decreases relatively rapidly at first and then more slowly?

5. Which graph shows a population that decreases relatively slowly at first and then more rapidly?

TEACHER NOTES

Students should complete Lessons 1.6 and 1.7 before you assign this lesson.

Exercise 1

Graph **c**; it illustrates the pattern that population growth often follows. As conditions become more crowded, growth slows. To help students appreciate the difference between graphs **b** and **c**, refer them to graphs **a** and **b** in Lesson 1.5, which show the populations increasing at slower and more rapid rates, respectively.

Exercise 2

Graph **b**; substances decay in this fashion. The process is rapid at first and then slows as time passes. To help students appreciate the difference between graphs **a** and **b**, refer them to the graphs in Lesson 1.7.

Exercise 3

Graph **a**; although graph **c** has the correct general shape, it has intervals of increase.

Exercise 4

Graph **a**; students might choose graph **d**, thinking in terms of a constant growth rate.

For each set of graphs, choose the one that best matches the situation. Write a sentence explaining your choice.

1. The population of Riverville increased at a rapid rate in the beginning and then leveled off as time passed.

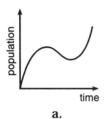
a.
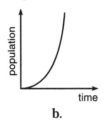
b.
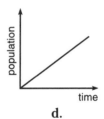
c.
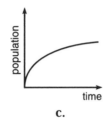
d.

2. The radioactive substance decayed rapidly at first and then decayed more slowly.

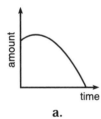
a.
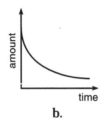
b.
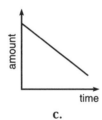
c.
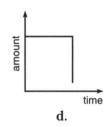
d.

3. The population of Mountaintop steadily decreased, reached an all-time minimum, and then began to grow.

a.
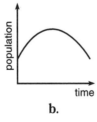
b.
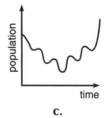
c.
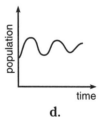
d.

4. The population of Spring Valley remained constant.

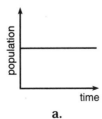
a.
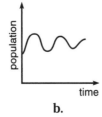
b.
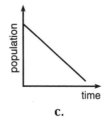
c.
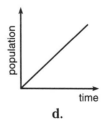
d.

TEACHER NOTES

Answers will vary. The best responses could be used as exercises for the entire class. It is suggested that you review with the students some of the relationships considered in Lessons 1.1–1.8. Time is often the quantity measured along the horizontal axis. The lessons have dealt with increasing and decreasing populations, cooling and decaying substances, and distance as a function of time. Also discussed were area and perimeter as a function of a square's side length and calories consumed as a function of grams of fudge eaten. Students might want to use height or weight as a function of age. This lesson is a good candidate for group work.

You have looked at several exercises in which a statement was made about a relationship between quantities and you chose the graph that matched the statement. Now make up your own exercise of this type. Write a statement about a relationship between quantities and give four possible graphs that could match the statement. Write a separate page of teacher notes for the exercise explaining why one particular graph is correct and why the other graphs are not.

Lessons 1.10 and 1.11 deal with various shape-based flasks that are being filled with water. In each case, the volume of water is being graphed along the horizontal axis and the height of the water is graphed along the vertical axis.

In Lesson 1.10, students need to realize that the narrower the container, the more quickly the water level will rise as water is added.

Exercise 1

Flask I matches graph **d**; flask II matches graph **c**; flask III matches graph **a**; and flask IV matches graph **b**. The widest flask matches the least steep line. The next narrower flask matches the next steeper line. The next narrower flask matches the next steeper line. Finally, the narrowest flask matches the steepest line. (With more advanced students, one can work directly with the formula $V = \pi r^2 h$ to see how the relationship between height and volume is affected by the radius of a cylinder.)

Exercise 2

A possible flask whose graph matches that of flask **III** is shown. Note that the radii of the three sections are the same.

Exercise 3

Here the flasks change radii twice, so each graph giving height as a function of volume will consist of three line segments. Again, smaller diameters will correspond to steeper line segments.

Flask **I** matches graph **c**; flask **II** matches graph **a**; flask **III** matches graph **d**; flask **IV** matches graph **b**.

Water is steadily dripped into each flask pictured below. The graphs describe the height of the water in the flask as a function of volume of water present. The graphs have the same scale along their axes.

1. Match each flask with a graph. Explain your reasoning.

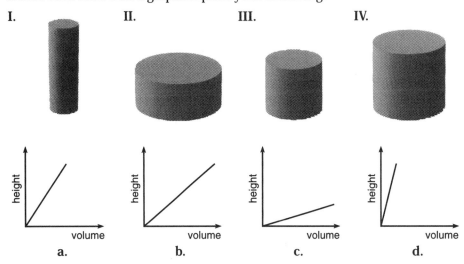

I. II. III. IV.

a. b. c. d.

2. Choose one of the flasks above and try to design a different flask which has the same graph.

3. Now consider the flasks below. Again match each flask with a graph. Explain your reasoning.

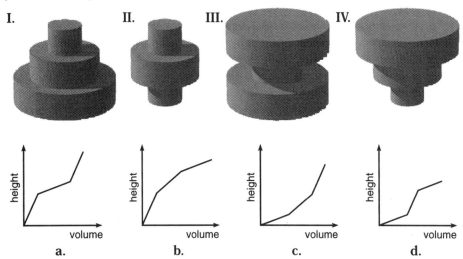

I. II. III. IV.

a. b. c. d.

This lesson should be done by only those students who have mastered Lesson 10 and want a greater challenge. The radius of each flask varies, with sections resembling a frustum of a right circular cone.

Exercise 1

Flask **I** matches graph **c**; flask **II** matches graph **d**; flask **III** matches graph **a**; flask **IV** matches graph **b**. (More advanced students should work with the formula for the frustum of a cone to see how the relationship between height and volume is affected by the radius.)

Exercise 2

Straight line segments on the graphs correspond to portions of the flask with constant radius. Sections of the graphs that are concave down indicate that the flasks are fanning out and the radii are increasing. Sections of the graphs that are concave up indicate that the flasks are becoming narrower and the radii are decreasing. A possible flask for each graph is shown.

a.   **b.**   **c.**   **d.**

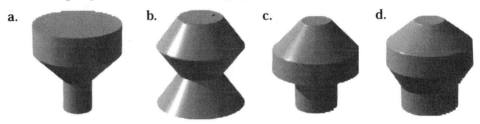

Once again water is steadily dripped into each flask pictured below. The graphs describe the height of the water in the flask as a function of volume of water present. The graphs have the same scale along their axes.

1. Match each flask with a graph. Explain your reasoning.

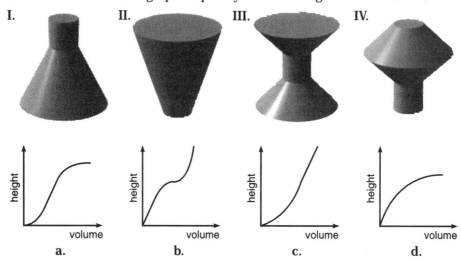

I. II. III. IV.

a. b. c. d.

2. Now consider the graphs below. Shetch a possible flask for each graph. Explain your reasoning.

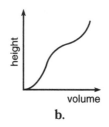
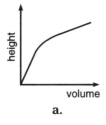
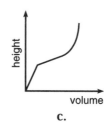
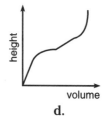

a. b. c. d.

Answers will vary. Have volunteers read their paragraphs and sketch their graphs on the chalkboard. This lesson is a good candidate for group work and lively discussion. You are also encouraged to make up your own exercises of this type for the class.

1. Janie spent an afternoon at the beach. The following graph shows her distance from the water as a function of time. Look at the graph and describe her afternoon. What did she do? Be sure your description matches the graph given.

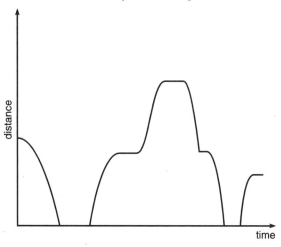

2. Janie spent another afternoon at the beach. Create a graph that shows her distance from the water as a function of time. Describe her afternoon. What did she do? This graph and its description should be different from those in Exercise 1. Be sure your description matches your graph.

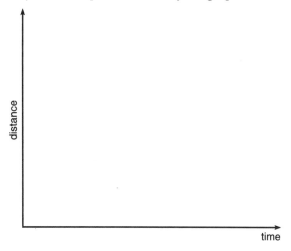

In Exercise 1, the students tell a story evoked by a sequence of four pictures. A happy or an unhappy event could be taking place. Students may decide that the player falls to the floor because he is ecstatic that he made the shot or because he is desolate that he did not. A crude graph of the action is all that is required for Exercise 2. A possible graph is given. For Exercise 3, students should then describe the up-and-down appearance of their graphs and how the graph relates to their description.

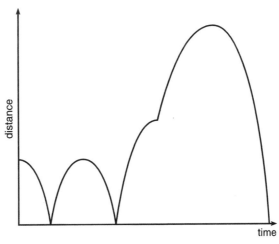

a.   b.   c.   d.

1. Write a few sentences describing what is happening in the sequence of pictures.

2. With your story in mind, graph the distance of the ball from the ground as a function of time.

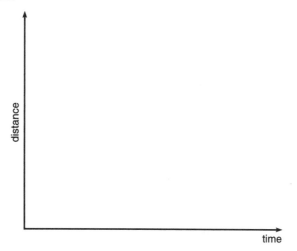

3. Write a few sentences explaining your graph.

This lesson is very similar to Lesson 1.13. In Exercise 1, the students tell a story evoked by a sequence of four pictures. A happy or an unhappy event could be taking place. Students may decide that the women part company as friends or because they are angry. A crude graph of the action is all that is required for Exercise 2. A possible graph is given. For Exercise 3, students should then describe the overall appearance of their graphs and how the graph relates to their description.

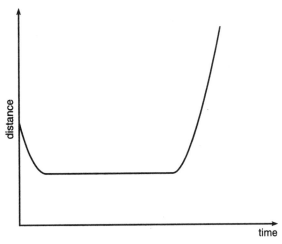

a.   b.   c.   d.

1. Write a few sentences describing what is happening in the sequence of pictures.

2. With your story in mind, graph the distance between the two women as a function of time.

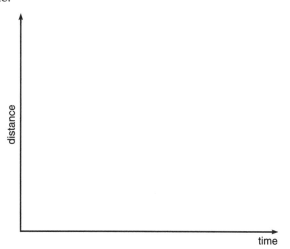

3. Write a few sentences explaining your graph.

Exercise 1

A possible graph is shown at the right. The horizontal segment indicates the time spent talking to the friend. In this portion of the graph, distance from home did not change.

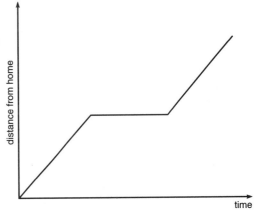

Exercise 2

A possible graph is shown at the right. It indicates that Bilbo fetched the stick five times.

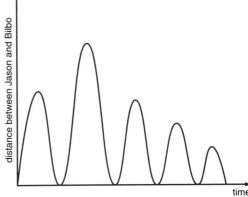

Exercise 3

A possible graph is shown at the right. It indicates that the trip home took half as long as the trip to the park.

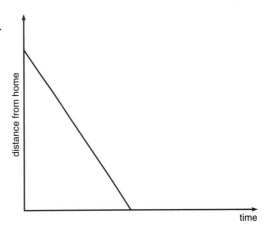

For each exercise, write a few sentences explaining your graph.

1. Jason took his dog Bilbo for a daily romp in the park. He walked slowly to the park, stopping to visit with a friend along the way. Graph his distance from home along the vertical axis and elapsed time along the horizontal axis. Be sure it is obvious from the graph that Jason stopped to visit with a friend. Remember that while Jason is standing with his friend he is not moving but time passes.

distance from home

time

2. At the park, Jason and Bilbo played a game of fetch. Jason threw a stick, and Bilbo retrieved it each time. Draw a graph with distance between Jason and Bilbo along the vertical axis and elapsed time along the horizontal axis.

distance between Jason and Bilbo

time

3. Jason and Bilbo ran home together. Again graph the distance from home along the vertical axis and elapsed time along the horizontal axis. Be sure it is obvious from the graph that the pair started out at the park and ended up at home. If the same amount of elapsed time is measured along the horizontal axis as in your graph for Exercise 1, show that the trip home took less time than the trip to the park.

distance from home

time

In discussing the graphs in this lesson, you may wish to introduce the terms *independent variable*, which is graphed along the horizontal axis, and *dependent variable*, which is graphed along the vertical axis.

Possible descriptions are given for all graphs.

Exercise 1

This graph describes something that increases and decreases in a periodic manner.

■ "A man rides on a Ferris wheel. The graph pictures the ride with *height above the ground* along the vertical axis and *time* along the horizontal axis."

■ "The graph shows the life cycle of a tree with the *number of leaves on the tree* along the vertical axis and *years* along the horizontal axis."

■ "The graph shows the rhythm of waves at a beach with *distance from a marker to the water line* along the vertical axis and *time* along the horizontal axis."

■ "The graph shows the orbits of two planets with *distance between the planets* along the vertical axis and *time* along the horizontal axis."

Exercise 2

Here the quantity measured along the vertical axis increases, then decreases, and then increases again, with the indication it will not decrease again.

■ "We set off on our trip but had to go back for a forgotten item and then set off again. The graph shows *distance from home* along the vertical axis and *time* along the horizontal axis."

With *time* measured along the horizontal axis, the vertical axis could represent quantities as diverse as *height above the ground, temperature,* or *stock price.*

■ "The kite rose in the air, came back down, and then rose again."

■ "The temperature rose, came back down, and then rose again."

■ "The stock price rose, then bottomed out, and then rose again."

Exercise 3

Here there is an increase and then a decrease. Again with *time* along the horizontal axis, there are many things that can be along the vertical axis.

■ "A firecracker was shot up into the air. *Height above the ground* is along the vertical axis."

■ "The temperature rose and then fell. *Temperature* is along the vertical axis."
There are examples in which time is not one of the quantities.

■ "As more and more money was spent on advertising, the profits first rose and then fell. *Amount spent* is along the horizontal axis, and *profits* are along the vertical axis."

■ "For a rectangle with a fixed perimeter as its width increases, the area first increases and then decreases. *Width* is along the horizontal axis, and *area* is along the vertical axis."

Consider the following graphs. Describe a situation that could be appropriately represented by each graph. Give the quantity measured along the horizontal axis as well as the quantity measured along the vertical axis.

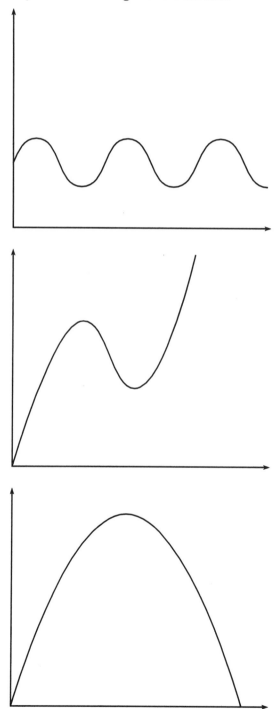

CHAPTER 2 UNDERSTANDING GRAPHS WITH SCALE

This chapter contains lessons similar to those in Chapter 1, but here the study of the graphs involves scale. While Chapter 1 focused on helping students to become comfortable with *qualitative* graphs, Chapter 2 focuses on helping students to become comfortable with *quantitative* graphs. Often the examples are the same as those encountered in high-school math courses. Exercises have been designed to make students aware of how different scales affect graphs. In addition, students must select the correct graph given several choices, interpret graphs, and draw their own graphs.

TEACHER NOTES

In this lesson, scale must be taken into account. It is a good lesson for the beginning of a first algebra course, as the types of graphs pictured are all part of that curriculum.

Exercise 1

Graph **d**; the rate does not change, so the function is linear and graphs **a**, **b**, and **d** are possible answers. Students should be encouraged to look at each graph very carefully and consider the amount earned after 2 hours. Graph **d** shows that after 2 hours, Derek will have earned $8.

Exercise 2

Graph **a**; there is no increase in the amount of money Monique has as she feeds in the quarters, so graphs **a** and **b** are the only possible answers. After playing 10 games, she will have $40.50 left. It is clear that graph **b** does not picture this.

Exercise 3

Graph **c**; as time goes by, the firecracker rises and then comes down. Students will encounter many projectile problems in the course of their math careers.

Exercise 4

Sample answer: Add scales to the graph as shown.

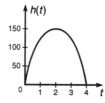

Exercise 5

Answers will vary. The graph should be a straight line, and the scale should be indicated.

1. Suppose Derek baby-sits and earns $4 per hour. Which of the following graphs shows the amount of money he will make after x hours of baby-sitting? Write a sentence explaining your choice.

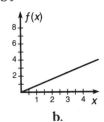
a.

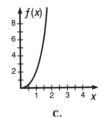
b.

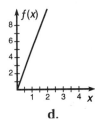
c.

d.

2. Monique starts out with $43 and heads for the video arcade. Which graph shows how much money she will have left after x games, assuming each game costs a quarter? Write a sentence explaining your choice.

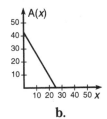
a.

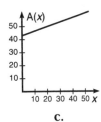
b.

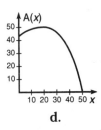
c.

d.

3. A firecracker is shot up into the sky. Which graph depicts its path through the air if time is measured along the horizontal axis and height above the ground is measured along the vertical axis? Write a sentence explaining your choice.

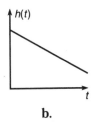
a.

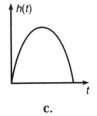
b.

c.

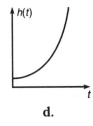
d.

4. Suppose you know that the maximum height of the firecracker in Exercise **3** is 150 feet, reached after two seconds. How could you indicate this information on the graph?

5. Reread Exercise 1. Think of a situation in which you might earn an hourly rate. Write a sentence describing it. Graph the amount of money you will earn after x hours of work.

Tell students that the £ stands for pounds, a British monetary unit.

Exercise 1

As the lines intersect around the year 1754, the level of imports was equal to the level of exports at this time. The amount for each was approximately £82,000.

Exercise 2

1725; about £102,000

Exercise 3

1700; about £70,000

Exercise 4

During the first 80 years of the eighteenth century, the level of imports varied between £70,000 and £102,000. This represents a range of only £32,000.

Exercise 5

The level of imports increased *and* decreased. From 1700 to 1725, the level of imports increased, then it decreased in the thirties, rose slightly in the forties, then decreased until 1760. Finally it increased again until 1780. The value of imports in 1700 was £70,000, while in 1780 it was £96,000. This represents a difference of £26,000.

Exercise 6

1780; about £186,000

Exercise 7

1700; about £35,000

Exercise 8

During the first 80 years of the eighteenth century, the level of exports varied between £35,000 and £186,000. This represents a range of £151,000, which is more than 4 times the range for imports.

Exercise 9

The level of exports increased *and* decreased. From 1700 to 1715, the level of exports increased, then it decreased until 1735, and finally it increased again until 1780. The value of exports was least in 1700, while the value of exports was greatest in 1780. Except for the 20-year span from 1715 to 1735, exports increased, sometimes rather dramatically.

Exercise 10

From 1750 to 1760, exports increased from £80,000 to £120,000. This averages to £4,000 per year. From 1760 to 1770, exports increased by about £22,000. This averages to £2,200 per year. When the graph is rising but looks linear like the graph for imports from 1700–1715, the rate of increase is steady. When the shape of the graph is a curve like the graph for exports from 1755–1760, the *rate* of increase becomes greater and greater. When the shape of the graph is a curve like the graph for exports from 1775–1780, the rate of increase becomes smaller and smaller.

Exercise 11

Sample answers: Exports increased dramatically from 1700 to 1780, while the increase in imports was relatively small. In 1700, imports were greater than exports; while in 1780, the reverse was true.

The graph on the next page illustrates a great deal about England's pattern of trade with Denmark and Norway during the first 80 years of the eighteenth century. Note that the vertical scale is in thousands of pounds (£).

1. When is the level of imports equal to the level of exports? What is true of the lines at this point? What was the value of each kind of trade?

2. In approximately which year was the level of imports greatest? What was the level of imports at this point?

3. In approximately which year was the level of imports least? What was the level of imports at this point?

4. Use your answers to Exercises 2 and 3 to find the difference between the two import levels. This difference is the *range of variation.*

5. As time passed, did the level of imports increase or decrease? Use the graph to describe what happened to the level of imports as time passed. Compare the level of imports in 1700 with the level in 1780.

6. In approximately which year was the level of exports greatest? What was the level of exports at this point?

7. In approximately which year was the level of exports least? What was the level of exports at this point?

8. Use your answers to Exercises 6 and 7 to find the difference between the two export levels. Compare this difference to the difference for imports in Exercise 4.

9. As time passed, did the level of exports increase or decrease? Use the graph to describe what happened to the level of exports as time passed. Compare the level of exports in 1700 with the level in 1780. Compare this answer to your answer in Exercise 5.

10. Often we want to look at the *rate* of change of increase or decrease in a particular graph. Study the levels of exports from 1750 to 1760 and again from 1770 to 1780. In which 10-year period, or *decade*, did the level increase faster? Sketch the graph for each decade, and make an observation about the shape of the curve. From 1755 to 1760, we say the rate of change increased; from 1775 to 1780, the rate of change decreased. Try to explain why.

11. Write two sentences comparing the imports and exports from 1700 to 1780.

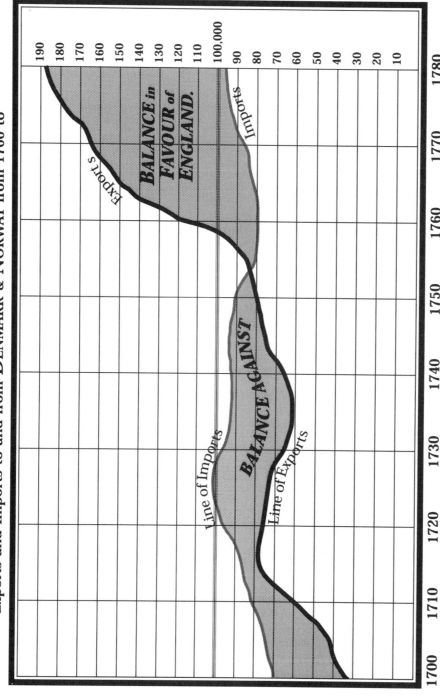

Exports and Imports to and from DENMARK & NORWAY from 1700 to

190
180
170
160
150
140
130
120
110
100,000
90
80
70
60
50
40
30
20
10

1700 1710 1720 1730 1740 1750 1760 1770 1780

Exports

BALANCE in
FAVOUR of
ENGLAND.

Imports

Line of Imports

BALANCE AGAINST

Line of Exports

The Bottom line is divided into Years, the Right hand line into £10,000

Published as the Act directs, 1st May, 1786, by Wᵐ Playfair

Neele sculpt 352.Strand, London

Source: Reprinted with permission from Edward R. Tufte's book, *The Visual Display of Quantitative Information.*

TEACHER NOTES

Exercise 1

Ted; about 22 seconds

Exercise 2

Jay

Exercise 3

After 6 seconds, 12 seconds, and 21 seconds

Exercise 4

After 6 seconds, about 30 yards; after 12 seconds, about 50 yards; after 21 seconds; about 83 yards

Exercise 5

A little over 14 seconds

Exercise 6

Jay, 80 yards; Ted, 60 yards

Exercise 7

From 2 to 5 seconds, Ted speeded up while Jay slowed down. When the curve has the shape ⌣ , the rate of change of distance with respect to time increases. When the curve has the shape ⌢ , the rate of change of distance with respect to time decreases.

Exercise 8

Answers will vary. Check students' graphs and descriptions.

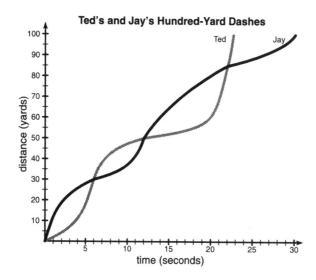

Ted's and Jay's Hundred-Yard Dashes

The graph above gives a rough sketch of the time it took Ted and Jay to run the 100-yard dash. Time in seconds is graphed along the horizontal axis and distance in yards is graphed along the vertical axis.

1. Who won the race? What was the winning time?

2. Who was ahead after five seconds?

3. At what time(s) were the contestants tied?

4. How far along the course were they when this happened?

5. How long did it take Jay to run 60 yards?

6. How far had the contestants run after 20 seconds?

7. Who speeded up and who slowed down from 2 to 5 seconds? Explain your reasoning.

8. Suppose you were a third contestant. Draw a curve to represent the course of your race and describe in words what happened. At 5 seconds, where were you in comparison to Ted and Jay? How long did it take you to run 50 yards? Indicate when you sped up, when you slowed down, and when you ran at a steady pace. Be sure what you write agrees with your graph.

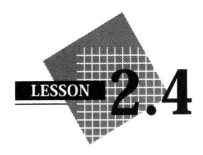

TEACHER NOTES

The exercises in Lessons 2.4 and 2.5 were first encountered in Chapter 1, Lessons 1.13 and 1.14.

In Exercise 1, Lesson 2.4, students tell a story evoked by a sequence of four pictures. A happy or a frustrating scene could be taking place. Students may decide that the player falls on the floor because he is ecstatic that he made the shot or because he is desolate that he did not. This time, students are asked to take scale into account. Their graphs will vary depending on the story given. Time can be measured in seconds along the *x*-axis and distance in feet along the *y*-axis. A possible graph is given for Exercise 2. This explanation for Exercise 3 is based on the graph given: the entire sequence takes 4 seconds. The ball is bounced twice, rising to a height of 4 feet, at $\frac{1}{2}$ second and $1\frac{1}{2}$ seconds. The ball is then shot at the basket, reaching a height of 12 feet at 3 seconds.

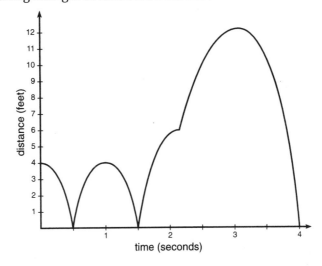

a.   b.   c.   d.

1. Write a few sentences describing what is happening in the sequence of pictures. If you did this exercise in Chapter 1, you may use the same idea you used before or come up with a new idea.

2. With your story in mind, graph the distance of the ball from the ground as a function of time. This time take scale into account. To get the proper scale for the x-axis, decide how long a period of time is needed for the action to take place. For the y scale, decide how high the ball goes.

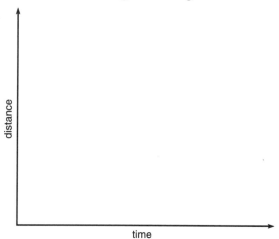

distance

time

3. Write a few sentences explaining your graph.

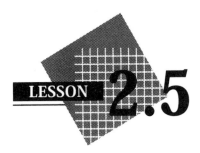

This lesson is very similar to Lesson 2.4. In Exercise 1, the students tell a story evoked by a sequence of four pictures. A happy or an unhappy event could be taking place. Students may decide that the women part company as friends or because they are angry. A possible graph is given for Exercise 2. For Exercise 3, students should then describe distances in relation to the time as shown on their graphs.

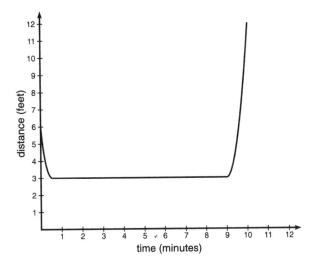

a.   b.   c.   d.

1. Write a few sentences describing what is happening in the sequence of pictures. If you did this exercise in Chapter 1, you may use the same idea you used before or come up with a new idea.

2. With your story in mind, graph the distance between the two women as a function of time. To get the proper scale for the *x*-axis, decide how long a period of time is needed for the action to take place. For the *y* scale, decide how far apart the two women are at each instant.

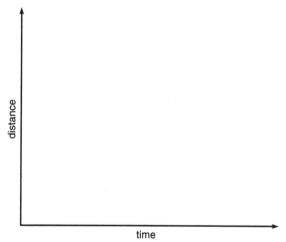

3. Write a few sentences explaining your graph.

LESSON 2.6 TEACHER NOTES

In this lesson and the next, students should see that different scales can radically change the look of the same graph. The appearance of a steep rise using a certain scale and a gentle one using another can lead to very different conclusions. It is clear that what is needed here is a sense of what constitutes a sharp rise in inflation in purely numerical terms.

Exercise 1

The impression given in Politician B's graph is that the rise of the price of coffee is very steep. A sample statement for the point (1992, 1.10) is, "In 1992, the average price for a cup of coffee was $1.10."

Exercise 2

The impression given in Politician A's graph is that the rise of the price of coffee is minimal. A sample statement for the point (1994, 1.20) is, "In 1994, the average price for a cup of coffee was $1.20."

Exercise 3

Yes

Exercise 4

Possible equation: $y = 0.05x - 98.5$

Extension

A good extension is to have the students make up their own situations similar to this one. They should think of a situations in which two people might want to take the same set of numbers and create opposite impressions with them.

Consider the following two graphs and the accompanying statements.

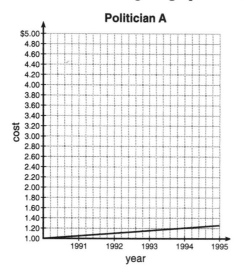

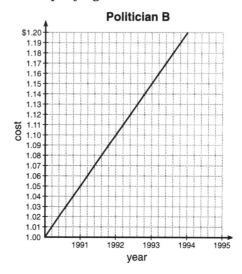

Politician A

My friends, I am honored to be here with you tonight and deeply desire to share my good news with each and every one of you. You need only look at the graph to comprehend my meaning. For the past five years, during my tenure in office, inflation has been very low. This means that the rise in the average price of a cup of coffee, for example, is a mere nickel a year, a nominal amount, a paltry sum. I trust I can count on your support in the upcoming election.

Politician B

My friends, I am honored to be here with you tonight and am happy to share the following information with each and every one of you. We are in crisis. Inflation is completely out of control. One need only look at my graph to see how bad the situation is. Look at the extraordinary rise in the average price of that ever-needed commodity, an ordinary cup of coffee. The rise is steep, off the charts, an undeserved burden on the American soul. It is clearly time for a change, and I trust I can count on your support in the upcoming election.

1. Study Politician B's graph. What is your impression of the rise of the price of coffee? Locate a point on the graph and use the information obtained from the point to write an appropriate statement about the price of a cup of coffee.

2. Study Politician A's graph. What is your impression of the rise of the price of coffee? Locate the same point on this graph that you chose in Exercise 1, and indicate its coordinates on the graph. Find a new point on this graph, and use the information obtained to write an appropriate statement about the price of a cup of coffee. Locate your second point on the other graph if you can.

3. Do the two lines represent the same set of points?

4. If you have studied algebra, write an equation for the graph of the lines.

TEACHER NOTES

Many teachers will have grown up using the same scale along both axes. With graphing calculators, students may use different scales along the axes. As in Lesson 2.6, the same increase appears both steep and gentle because of the scale chosen. In Exercise 1, graphs **b**, **c**, and **d** are all valid representations for $y = 10x$. In graph **c** the line rises steeply, while in graph **d** the line rises very gently.

Exercise 1

Graph **a** is not a valid representation for $y = 10x$, as (20, 40) is a point on the graph and $40 \neq 10 \times 20$. This graph looks exactly like graph **c**, which is a valid representation. Students should use the scales on each graph to check whether the representation is valid.

Exercise 2

Although the graphs look the same, graph **c** is not a valid representation for $y = 5x$ as (1, 1) is a point on the graph and $1 \neq 5 \times 1$.

Exercise 3

We know that $y = x^2$ passes through (0, 0), so graph **c** cannot represent the curve. The other three graphs can. If graphing calculators are available, students should use different scales and create graphs for $y = x^2$ that look like graphs **a**, **b**, and **c**.

Exercise 4

This exercise is designed for students who are taking algebra. They should note that axis scales are not necessary. The line in graph **a** has negative slope and positive y-intercept, so it matches $y = -6x + 3$, which is the only equation for a line with negative slope and positive y-intercept. The line in graph **b** has positive slope and negative y-intercept, so it matches $4.1x - 3y = 5$, which is the only equation for a line with positive slope and negative y-intercept. The line in graph **c** has positive slope and positive y-intercept, so it matches $-2y + 3x + 5 = 0$, which is the only equation for a line with positive slope and positive y-intercept. The line in graph **d** has negative slope and negative y-intercept, so it matches $-2x - 6y = 8$, which is the only equation for a line with negative slope and negative y-intercept.

1. Which of the following graphs could *not* be a representation for $y = 10x$? Explain why.

a.

b.

c.

d.

2. Which of the following could *not* be a representation for $y = 5x$? Explain why.

a.

b.

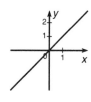

c.

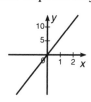

d.

3. Which of the following could *not* be a representation for $y = x^2$? Explain why.

a.

b.

c.

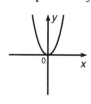

d.

4. Match each graph with one of the equations below. Explain your choices.

a.

b.

c.

d.

$y = -6x + 3$ $-2y + 3x + 5 = 0$ $4.1x - 3y = 5$ $-2x - 6y = 8$

 **LESSON 2.8**

TEACHER NOTES

This lesson presents a graph that corresponds to a verbal statement. Students must take scale into account in order to answer the questions relating to the situation. They are asked to think about what the horizontal line segment represents and what it means in terms of this situation for one line to be steeper than another.

Exercise 1

55 miles

Exercise 2

200 miles

Exercise 3

110 miles

Exercise 4

260 miles

Exercise 5

290 miles

Exercise 6

2 hours

Exercise 7

A half unit long; Carol's time resting

Exercise 8

3 hours

Exercise 9

5 hours

Exercise 10

The segment corresponding to hours, 0–2; the segment corresponding to hours, 2.5–5.5; the second line is steeper as Carol is driving at a faster rate.

Carol drove her car at an average rate of 55 miles per hour for 2 hours. She stopped driving for a half hour to rest and then drove for 3 hours longer at an average rate of 60 miles per hour. In the graph below, time in hours is along the horizontal axis and distance in miles is along the vertical axis. The graph represents Carol's trip. Study the graph carefully, and then use the information from above and from the graph to answer the questions.

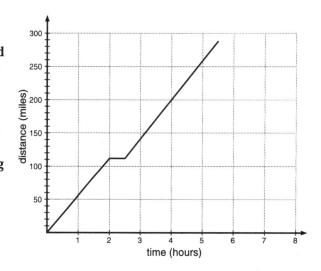

How many miles had Carol traveled

1. after 1 hour?

2. after 4 hours?

3. after 2.5 hours?

4. after 5 hours?

5. How many miles did Carol travel in all?

6. After how many hours had Carol traveled 110 miles?

7. How long is the horizontal segment on the graph and what does it represent in terms of Carol's trip?

8. After how many hours had Carol traveled 140 miles?

9. How long was Carol driving?

10. Point out the segment that is used to calculate the distance traveled for the first 2 hours of the trip. Point out the segment that is used to calculate the distance traveled for the last 3 hours of the trip. Is one line steeper than the other? If so, which one and why?

TEACHER NOTES

Exercise 1

30 mph for $1\frac{1}{2}$ hours; total distance of $30 \times 1.5 = 45$ miles

Exercise 2

Nathan took a half-hour break.

Exercise 3

55 mph for 2 hours; total additional distance of $55 \times 2 = 110$ miles; total distance of $45 + 110 = 155$ miles

Exercise 4

65 mph for $2\frac{1}{2}$ hours; total additional distance of $65 \times 2.5 = 162.5$ miles; total distance of $155 + 162.5 = 317.5$ miles

Exercise 5

Descriptions will vary.

Exercise 6

(1.5, 45); a possible statement is, "After $1\frac{1}{2}$ hours, Nathan had traveled 45 miles." Slope of the segment is $\frac{45-0}{1.5-2} = 30$; slope is the same as the speed.

Exercise 7

(1.5, 45) and (2, 45), so the slope is $\frac{45-45}{2-1.5} = 0$; no distance was covered during this half hour; a possible statement is, "After 2 hours, Nathan had traveled 45 miles."

Exercise 8

Remind students that change in y over change in x gives *speed* as well as *slope*, as y is distance and x is time. (2, 45) and (4, 155), so the slope is $\frac{155-45}{4-2} = 55$; a possible statement is, "After 4 hours, Nathan had traveled 155 miles."

Exercise 9

(4, 155) and (6.5, 317.5), so the slope is $\frac{317.5-155}{6.5-4} = 65$; a possible statement is, "After $6\frac{1}{2}$ hours, Nathan had traveled a total of 317.5 miles."

Exercise 10

$\frac{317.5}{6.5} \approx 48.85$ mph

Exercise 11

$f(x) = 30x, 0 < x < 1.5$
$f(x) = 45, 1.5 < x < 2$
$f(x) = 55x - 65, 2 < x < 4$
$f(x) = 65x - 105, 4 < x < 6.5$

The equations for these lines are obtained using the endpoints and the standard method for finding the equation of a line given two points.

Nathan took a trip and carefully monitored his speed for $6\frac{1}{2}$ hours. At the right is a graph giving his speed as a function of time. Time in hours is along the horizontal axis, and speed in miles per hour is along the vertical axis.

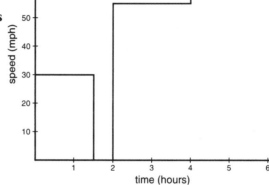

1. When Nathan began to monitor his speed, how fast was he going and how long did he continue at this speed? How many miles did he travel at this speed?

2. What happened next? How long did this last?

3. At what speed did Nathan next travel, and how long did he remain at this speed? How many miles did he travel at this speed? What was the total number of miles Nathan had traveled since he began monitoring?

4. What was Nathan's final speed, and how long did he travel at that speed? What was the total number of miles traveled at this speed? What was the total number of miles traveled in all?

5. Try to imagine where Nathan went on this trip and what accounted for the different variations in speed. Write a description of this trip.

At the right is a graph showing the total distance that Nathan traveled as a function of time. Time in hours is along the horizontal axis, and distance in miles is along the vertical axis. The graph is a series of connected line segments, with each line segment corresponding to a different speed. For each point (*x*, *y*) on this graph, you can make a statement about the trip, namely, that after *x* hours you have traveled a total of *y* miles.

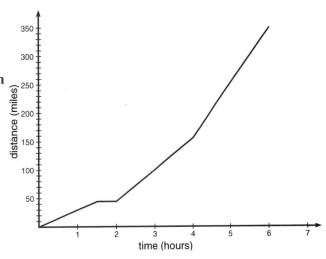

For Exercises 6–11, use the information above and the information at the top of page 56.

6. For the segment whose one endpoint is (0, 0), give the coordinates of the other endpoint. Make a statement about the trip using the information given by this point. Consider these two endpoints. The *slope* of this segment is the difference in the *y*-coordinates divided by the difference in the *x*-coordinates. Find the slope. How is the slope related to the speed?

7. Give the endpoints of the second segment and use them to find the slope of the segment. Make a statement about the trip using the information given by the right-hand endpoint.

8. Predict the slope for the third segment. Then give its endpoints and calculate its slope. Make a statement about the trip using the information given by the right-hand endpoint.

9. Predict the slope for the fourth segment. Then give its endpoints and calculate its slope. Make a statement about the trip using the information given by the right-hand endpoint.

10. Use the formula *distance* = *rate* × *time* to find the average speed for the entire trip.

11. If you have had algebra, give the algebraic representation of this piecewise function by finding an equation for each segment and giving the proper restrictions for the *x* values.

Exercise 1

20 mph for $\frac{1}{2}$ hour; total distance of 10 miles

Exercise 2

70 mph for 2 hours; total additional distance of 140 miles; total distance of 150 miles

Exercise 3

Allison took a half-hour break.

Exercise 4

50 mph for 2 hours; total additional distance of 100 miles; total distance of 250 miles

Exercise 5

Descriptions will vary.

Exercise 6

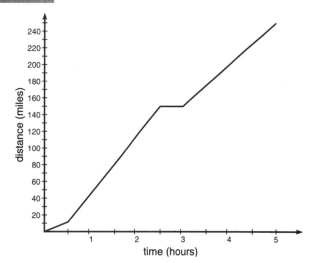

Exercise 7

This period of time corresponds to a horizontal segment on the graph.

Exercise 8

First segment slope, 20; second segment slope, 70; third segment slope, 0; fourth segment slope, 50; each slope corresponds to the speed for that portion of the journey.

Allison took a trip and carefully monitored her speed for 5 hours. At the right is a graph giving her speed as a function of time. Time in hours is along the horizontal axis, and speed in miles per hour is along the vertical axis.

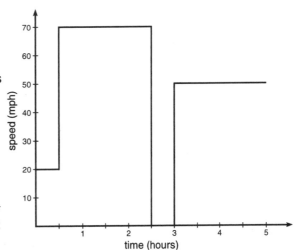

1. When Allison began to monitor, how fast was she going and how long did she continue at this speed? How many miles did she travel at this speed?

2. To what speed did Allison shift, and how long did she remain at this speed? How many miles did she travel at this speed? What was the total number of miles Allison traveled since she began monitoring?

3. What happened next? How long did this last?

4. What was Allison's final speed, and how long did she travel at that speed? What was the total number of miles traveled at this speed? What was the total number of miles traveled in all?

5. Try to imagine where Allison went on this trip and what accounted for the different variations in speed. Write a description of this trip.

6. Now graph total distance traveled as a function of time on the grid at the right.

Use your answers from Exercises 1–4.

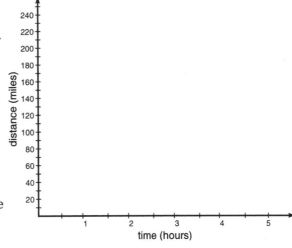

7. How is the period of time when the car was stopped indicated on the graph you drew?

8. If you have had algebra, give the slope of each line segment on your graph.

Exercise 1

(1, 45); "After 1 hour, Mr Anderson had gone 45 miles." The slope is 45. A possible statement is, "Mr. Anderson traveled at 45 mph for 1 hour."

Exercise 2

(1, 45) and (1.5, 45), so the slope is 0; no distance was covered during this half hour; a possible statement is, "Mr. Anderson did not drive for a half hour."

Exercise 3

(1.5, 45) and (3, 142.5), so the slope is 65; a possible statement is, "Mr. Anderson traveled at 65 mph for $1\frac{1}{2}$ hours."

Exercise 4

(3, 142.5) and (4, 172.5), so the slope is 30; a possible statement is, "Mr. Anderson traveled at 30 mph for 1 hour."

Exercise 5

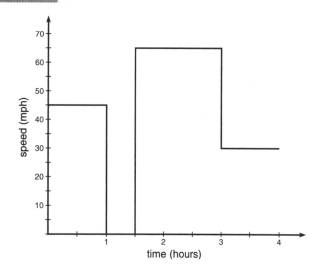

Exercise 6

Descriptions will vary.

Exercise 7

$f(x) = 45x, 0 < x < 1$
$f(x) = 45, 1 < x < 1.5$
$f(x) = 65x - 52.5, 1.5 < x < 3$
$f(x) = 30x + 52.5, 3 < x < 4$

Mr. Anderson took a trip and for 4 hours carefully monitored the total distance traveled after each change in speed. At the right is a graph giving his distance traveled as a function of time.

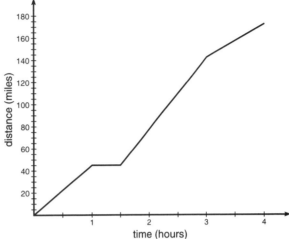

1. Give the coordinates of the right-hand endpoint for the first segment. Make a statement about the trip using the information given by this point. Use both endpoints of the segment to find its slope. Use the slope to tell how fast Mr. Anderson was traveling on the first leg of his trip. How long did he maintain that speed?

2. Give the endpoints of the second segment and use them to find its slope. Make a statement about the next leg of the trip using the information given by the slope and the difference between the *x*-coordinates of the endpoints.

3. Give the endpoints of the third segment and use them to find its slope. Make a statement about the trip using the information given by the slope and the difference between the *x*-coordinates of the endpoints.

4. Give the endpoints of the fourth segment and use them to find its slope. Make a statement about the trip using the information given by the slope and the difference between the *x*-coordinates of the endpoints.

5. Now graph speed as a function of time on the grid at the right. Use your answers for Exercises 1–4.

6. Try to imagine where Mr. Anderson went on this trip and what accounted for the different variations in speed. Write a description of this trip.

7. If you have studied piecewise functions, give the algebraic representation for the graph in Exercise 1–4.

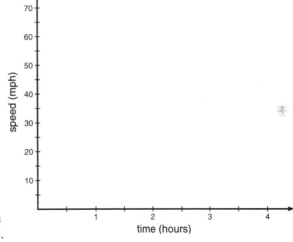

© Addison-Wesley Publishing Company, Inc./ Published by Dale Seymour Publications®

LESSON 2.12 TEACHER NOTES

Exercise 1

No; the graph shows that his speed drops to 0 mph only three times, and there are three stop signs.

Exercise 2

After about $3\frac{1}{2}$ minutes, because the curve is highest at that time; about 4 blocks

Exercise 3

The speed is 0 mph for horizontal segments on the graph.

Exercise 4

Possible description: Teddy had the speed up to 10 mph, and then he stopped for the first stop sign. He sped up to 15 mph on the second block before stopping and turning. He drove down Whitney Avenue, reaching a maximum of 30 mph and slowing down to go around the curve. He stopped at the stop sign and reached a maximum of 10 mph on the last block, slowing down to enter the parking lot.

Exercise 5

Answers will vary.

Teddy lives eight blocks from school. The diagram at the right shows Teddy's route from home to school. The drive takes only 7 minutes.

Below the diagram are two graphs corresponding to one of Teddy's trips to school. The first shows the speed of the car as a function of time, and the second shows the number of blocks traveled as a function of time.

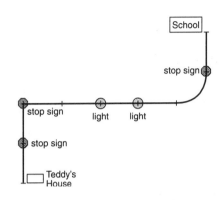

1. Assuming he obeyed the law at all times, did Teddy have to stop for any lights? Explain.

2. When was Teddy driving the fastest? How do you know? How many blocks had Teddy traveled at that time?

3. Explain how you can tell from the second graph when Teddy's speed is zero miles per hour.

4. Describe Teddy's trip. Refer to the graphs and the diagram.

5. Draw a map of the route you take from your house to your school. Then graph the speed of your trip as a function of time.

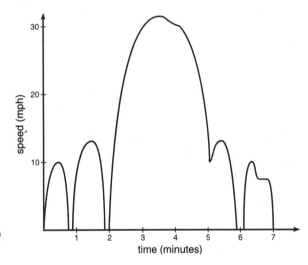

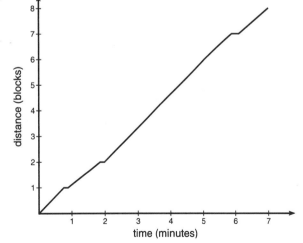

Exercise 1

Students' descriptions should refer to José's making two short stops at the beginning and end of the outing and three longer stops of the appropriate length. The first two short horizontal line segments may indicate that two friends were picked up to join the group. The last two horizontal line segments may indicate these friends were dropped off, as the distance from home is the same.

Exercise 2

Answers will vary. Check to see that students' graphs correspond to their stories.

Exercise 3

Answers will vary. Check to see that students' graphs correspond to their stories.

1. José went out with a group of friends. The graph at the right gives his distance from home as a function of time. Write a description of where José went, what he did, and how long he stayed at each place. Be sure your statements match the graph.

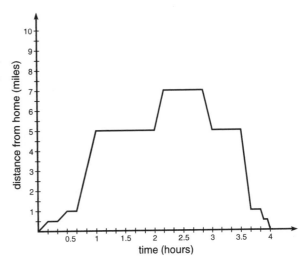

2. Think of a time you went out with a group of friends. Describe where you went, what you did, and how long you stayed there. On the grid at the right, draw a graph that matches your statements, giving your distance from home as a function of time.

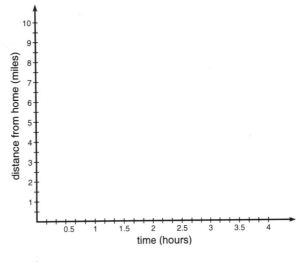

3. On the grid at the right, draw a graph indicating your distance from your bed as a function of time as you follow your normal morning routine. Describe where you are in your house, what you are doing, and how long you stay in that room. Be sure your statements match the graph.

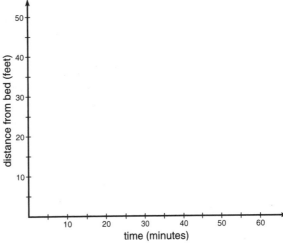

In this lesson, students must identify correct graphs as they did in Chapter 1, but now they must provide a scale based on the information given in the description of the situation.

Exercise 1

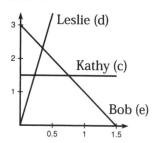

Exercise 2

2 mph (distance 3 divided by time $1\frac{1}{2}$)

Exercise 3

6 mph

Exercise 4

0 mph

Exercise 5

3 times as fast

Exercise 6

Since Kathy was standing still, the question makes no sense.

Exercise 7

No; the slopes of the lines have nothing to do with the slope of the road.

Exercise 8

Yes; after $\frac{3}{8}$ hour, at which time Bob had gone $\frac{3}{4}$ mile and Leslie had gone $2\frac{1}{4}$ miles. Algebraically, where t = time, Bob's distance is $2t$ and Leslie's distance is $6t$; since the distance between the two is 3 miles, $2t + 6t = 3$, and $t = \frac{3}{8}$.

Exercise 9

Yes; Leslie, because the slope of her graph is steeper than the slope of Bob's graph; she traveled the same distance in less time.

Exercise 10

$\frac{2}{3}$ of the trip from the station to the library; after $\frac{3}{4}$ hour. Algebraically, the time when Bob passed Kathy can be found by solving the equation $2x = 1.5$. (Bob's distance must be 1.5 miles in order to reach Kathy; $2x$, his rate times the time, represents his distance.) Leslie passed Kathy after $\frac{1}{4}$ hour. (Leslie's distance must be 1.5 miles in order to reach Kathy; $6x$, her rate times the time, represents her distance.)

Bob left the train station and walked at a slow, steady pace toward the library, which is 3 miles down the road. He reached the library in $1\frac{1}{2}$ hours. At the same time Bob left the station, Leslie left the library and ran down the road at a steady pace toward the train station, reaching the station in $\frac{1}{2}$ hour. Kathy was standing on the road midway between the library and the train station. She greeted Bob and Leslie as each went by. In the graphs below, distance from the library is along the vertical axis while time is along the horizontal axis. The moment when Leslie and Bob started out is at zero.

a.
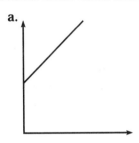

b.
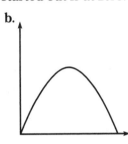

c.
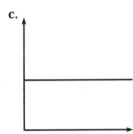

d.
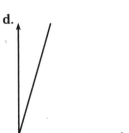

e.
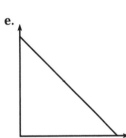

f.
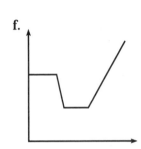

1. Decide which of the 6 graphs above describes each person's location in relation to time. Then draw the graph for each person on the grid at the right, using an appropriate scale.

2. What was Bob's speed in miles per hour?

3. What was Leslie's speed in miles per hour?

4. What was Kathy's speed in miles per hour?

5. How many times as fast as Bob was Leslie going?

6. Explain whether it makes sense to ask this question: "How many times as fast as Kathy was Leslie moving?"

7. Can you conclude that the train station is uphill from the library? Explain.

8. Did Bob and Leslie meet? If so, find when they met and how far each had traveled at that time. If you have studied algebra, give an equation that can be used to represent the problem.

9. Can you tell from the graph who traveled faster? Explain your answer.

10. What portion of the trip from the station to the library had Bob completed after 1 hour? When did he pass Kathy? When did Leslie pass Kathy?

This is a good lesson for students who are being introduced to the coordinate plane and who have had some experience with the Distance Formula. The class should discuss the fact that after 1 unit of time, the person who is walking fastest will have covered the greatest distance. For each line, ask how many units of distance have been covered during 1 unit of time. This discussion should enable the class to complete the exercises.

Exercise 1

It is clear that lines **c**, **d**, and **e** correspond to the 3 students who start at the tower, since their distance from the tower is 0 at the outset. Students should be able to reason that after 1 unit of time, Leslie has gone the farthest and Bob has gone the least distance. Therefore, Leslie's walk is represented by line **e**, Kathy's by line **d**, and Bob's by line **c**. Similarly, as Dave covers less distance in each unit of time than Ann does, line **a** corresponds to Ann and line **b** to Dave.

Exercise 2

Students should note that the steeper the line, the faster the person walked; the less steep the line, the slower the person walked. Students should also be able to order the people's speeds by considering the distances covered in 1 unit of time. Leslie was walking fastest and Dave slowest. No two people walked at the same speed.

Exercise 3

Leslie: 3 meters per second; Kathy: 1 meter per second; Bob: $\frac{1}{2}$ meter per second; Ann: 2 meters per second; and Dave: 0.3 meter per second

Exercise 4

Each person's speed is now doubled; Leslie: 6 meters per second; Kathy: 2 meters per second; Bob: 1 meter per second; Ann: 4 meters per second; and Dave: 0.6 meter per second

Exercise 5

Using the conversion 1 in. = 2.54 cm, 1 mi = 1609.344 m and 3 miles per hour corresponds to $\frac{3}{60^2}$ miles per second, which translates to 1.34112 meters per second.

Exercise 6

Students' paragraphs will vary. They should indicate that steepness, or slope, can determine how people's speeds are related, but that a scale is necessary for calculating a rate. They might say that using the same scale for time but varying the scale for distance will show different rates. Exercises 3 and 4 illustrate how different scales lead to different rates.

Leslie, Bob, and Kathy all left Altgeld Science Tower at 3:30. Of the three, Leslie was walking the fastest and Bob the slowest. At the same time, Dave and Ann were walking toward the tower, although Dave was walking more slowly than Ann. In the graph at the right, each person's walk is represented by one of the lines. Time is along the horizontal axis, and distance is along the vertical axis.

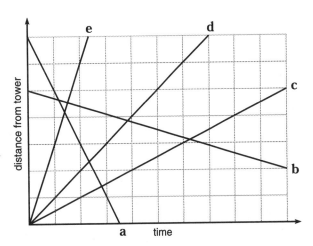

1. Identify which line should be associated with each person.

2. Who was walking fastest? Who was walking slowest? Are any two walking at the same speed?

3. If each grid mark along the horizontal axis represents 1 second and each grid mark along the vertical axis represents 1 meter, how fast is each person walking?

4. If each grid mark along the horizontal axis represents a half second and each grid mark along the vertical axis represents 1 meter, how fast is each person walking?

5. Many people walk at the rate of 3 miles per hour. How many meters per second is this? (1 inch = 2.54 centimeters)

6. Suppose you are given a graph similar to the one above, with no scale indicated. Write a paragraph explaining why you can say a certain person is walking faster than another but you cannot say someone is walking fast. Give different scales to illustrate your point.

This is an amazing piece of graphical design, and you are encouraged to make up your own questions concerning it. Students will need centimeter rulers to complete the exercises.

Exercise 1

10 minutes

Exercise 2

The length of the vertical line from Paris to Lyon is 10 cm and from Paris to Dijon is 6.2 cm. The proportion $\frac{6.2}{10} = \frac{D}{512}$ can be solved, giving 317.44 km as the approximate distance between Paris and Dijon. With the conversion 1 kilometer = 0.621 mile, the distance is about 197.13 miles.

Exercise 3

6:30 A.M.; there is no break in the line at Moret, so the train spent no time there; the short horizontal segment in the line at Montereau indicates a 5-minute stop at the station; from Montereau, the train went to Laroche and stopped for 10 minutes; it then went to Tonnerre and stopped for 30 minutes; at both Nuits and Raviere, it stopped for 5 minutes and then went on to Dijon.

Exercise 4

5 A.M.; the trains met between Lac Laumes and Dijon at about 1:35 P.M.; you might have chosen to take the 6:55 train, as it was faster.

Exercise 5

If Henri had left Paris at 11 A.M., he would have arrived in Lyon at 10:10 P.M. This trip took 11 hours 10 minutes, so his average rate was about $\frac{512}{11.2}$ kilometers per hour, which is about 45.7 km/h or about 28.4 mph.

Exercise 6

If Henri had missed the 11:00 train, he would have taken the 12:20 train and arrived in Lyon at 6:05 A.M. This trip took 17 hours 45 minutes, for an average rate of about 28.8 km/h or about 17.9 mph. The steeper the slope of the line, the faster the train.

Exercise 7

7:15 P.M. train; it arrived at 4:35 A.M., taking 9 hours 20 minutes.

Exercise 8

The 1981 express took $\frac{9.3}{3}$ hours, or just over 3 times as fast as the fastest 1885 train. The path of this 1981 train begins at the top of the chart at 8 A.M. and goes straight down to 11 A.M. along the bottom.

Exercise 9

Students' questions will vary.

The intriguing graphic on the following page, created by E. J. Marey in 1885, gives the train schedule for Paris to Lyon. Time is indicated along the horizontal axis, while the stations are separated in proportion to their actual distance apart along the vertical axis. **Midi** is noon in French and **minuit** is midnight.

1. What unit of time is represented between two vertical lines?

2. The distance from Paris to Lyon is 512 kilometers (km). About how far is it from Paris to Dijon? Give your answer in kilometers and in miles.
   (1 kilometer = 0.621 mile)

3. At what time did the earliest train leave Paris for Lyon? It appears that this train did not stop in Moret; explain why. Describe the train's journey as far as Dijon, indicating how long it stopped at each station.

4. What time did the earliest train leave Lyon for Paris? Where and when did this train meet the train from Paris to Lyon? Why might you decide to not take the earliest train from Lyon to Paris?

5. If Henri left Paris at 11:00 A.M., what was the earliest time he could have reached Lyon? What was his average rate for this trip? Give the rate in both kilometers and miles per hour.

6. Suppose Henri missed the 11:00 A.M. train and was forced to take the next train. What was the earliest time he could have reached Lyon in this case? What was his average rate for this trip? How can you tell from the slopes of the lines that correspond to the trains which trip is quicker?

7. Which train from Paris to Lyon is fastest?

8. In 1981, the express train from Paris to Lyon was scheduled to leave Paris at 8 A.M. and to take only 3 hours. Graph the path of this train on the 1885 schedule. This train is how many times as fast as the fastest 1885 train?

9. Study the schedule and think of questions concerning it. Write three different types of questions.

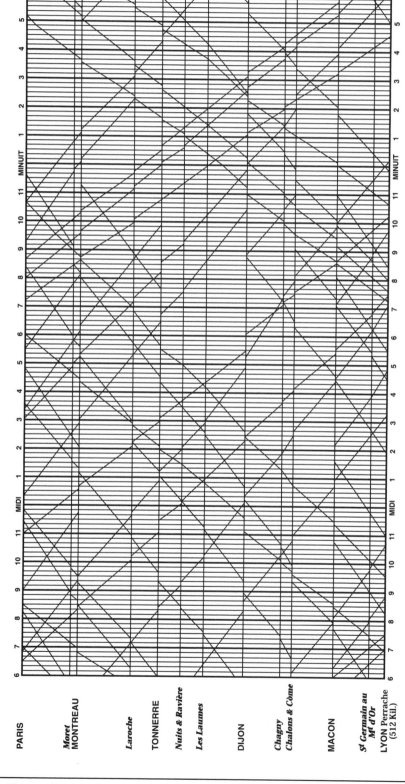

PARIS

Moret
MONTREAU

Laroche

TONNERRE

Nuits & Ravière

Les Laumes

DIJON

Chagny
Chalons & Còme

MACON

St Germain au
Mt d'Or
LYON Perrache
(512 Kil.)

Source: Reprinted with permission from Edward R. Tufte's book, *The Visual Display of Quantitative Information.*

The correct graph is shown on the next page. Students' questions and answers will vary.

You might want to give students copies of this graph and ask some of the following questions if students have not included them.

Exercise 1

Horizontal lines are indicated to mark the stations. How can you tell which leg of the journey is the shortest? (The shortest distance between two horizontal lines is from Raleigh to Burlington.)

Exercise 2

How can you check the answer you gave for Exercise 1 numerically? (Find the difference of the two cities' distances from New York. The distance between Raleigh and Burlington, 590 – 530 = 60, is the least.)

Exercise 3

How can you tell from your graph which leg of the journey is the longest? (The longest distance between two horizontal lines is from New York to Washington.)

Exercise 4

How can you check the answer you gave for Exercise 3 numerically? (Find the difference of the two cities' distances from New York. The distance between New York and Washington, 225 – 0 = 225, is the greatest.)

Exercise 5

How can you tell from your graph where the train stops for the longest time? (Find the longest horizontal segment in either train's course; the longest is at Washington on the Burlington-Washington run.) How can you check this numerically? (Subtract the appropriate time intervals on the horizontal axis or refer to the original schedule.)

Exercise 6

How can you tell from your graph on which leg the train's average rate is fastest? (The steeper the slope of the line segment, the faster the train is going.) How can you check this numerically? (For each segment, find the change in distance divided by change in time.)

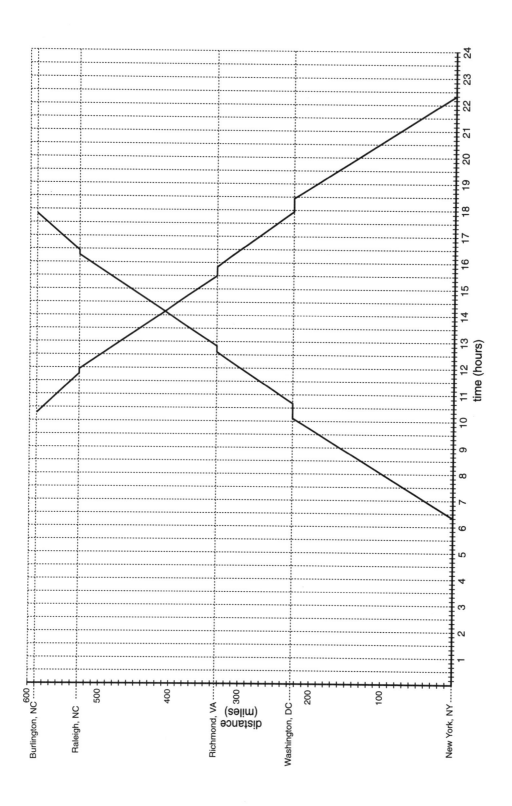

Study the Amtrak train schedule for the train from New York to Burlington, North Carolina, on the accompanying page. On the grid below, place New York, Washington, Richmond, Raleigh, and Burlington along the vertical axis, separated in proportion to their actual distance apart. The horizontal axis is labeled by hours with 10-minute intervals. Chart the course of each train. Write four questions concerning your graph. Provide an answer key.

AMTRAK'S

Carolinian

Spring 1995 Effective April 2

New York...Washington...Richmond...Raleigh...Burlington

79			◄ Train Number ►			80
Daily			◄ Days of Operation ►			**Daily**
ReadDown	Mile	▼		Symbol	▲	Read Up
67/77			*Connecting Train Number*			*66/76*
9 35P	*0*	Dp	*Boston, MA–South Sta.* ✹ *(ET)*	🚬⊘♿	Ar	*8 21A*
R *10 38P*	*44*	⬇	*Providence, RI* ✹	⊘♿	Ar	*7 21A*
1 09A	*156*		*New Haven, CT*	⊘♿	Ar	*4 40A*
7 55A	*457*	Ar	*Washington, DC* ✹	🚬⊘♿	Dp	49
6 20A	0	Dp	New York, NY--Penn Sta. ✹ (ET)	🚬📞♿	Ar	10 22P
R 6 36A	10		Newark, NJ--Penn Sta. 12	📞♿		D 9 59P
6 51A	25		Metropark, NJ	♿ 31		D 9 44P
7 13A	49		Princeton Jct., NJ (Princeton Jct. 38)	⊘♿ 31		9 27P
7 23A	58		Trenton, NJ	🚬📞♿		9 18P
7 49A	86		North Philadelphia, PA			
8 08A	91		Philadelphia, PA--30th St. Sta. 8 ✹	🚬📞♿		8 43P
8 30A	116		Wilmington, DE	🚬📞♿		8 11P
9 22A	185		Baltimore, MD--Penn Sta. ✹	🚬📞♿		7 17P
9 35A	196		BWI Airport Rail Sta., MD 7	♿		7 01P
9 50A	216		New Carrollton, MD	📞♿		6 45P
10 05A / 10 35A	225	Ar / Dp	Washington, DC ✹	🚬📞♿	Dp / Ar	6 35P / 5 55P
10 50A	233		Alexandria, VA	📞♿		5 30P
✹11 07A	249		Woodbridge, VA	●		
✹11 18A	260		Quantico, VA	●		✹ 4 57P
✹11 36A	279	⬇	Fredericksburg, VA	●		✹ 4 37P
12 35P / 12 50P	334	Ar / Dp	Richmond, VA ✹	📞♿	Dp / Ar	3 50P / 3 30P
1 22P	363	Ar	Petersburg, VA	📞	Dp	2 37P
2 47P	460	Dp	Rocky Mount, NC	📞♿	Ar	1 17P
3 05P	477	⬇	Wilson, NC	●	⬆	1 00P
3 30P	502		Selma-Smithfield, NC	●		12 34P
4 17P / 4 27P	530	Ar / Dp	Raleigh, NC	📞♿	Dp / Ar	11 55A / 11 45A
5 05P	556		Durham, NC (Chapel Hill)	●		11 05A
5 49P	590	Ar	Burlington, NC	●	Dp	10 19A

Connecting Services

🚌 Amtrak Thruway Bus Connection—Greensboro, NC/Winston-Salem, NC						
36	0	Dp	Greensboro, NC		Ar	9 20A
7 45P	30	Ar	Winston-Salem, NC--Old Salem Inn	●	Dp	8 35A

Services on the Carolinian

Coaches—Reservations required (except locally between New York and Washington)

Dinette—New York–Charlotte—Sandwiches, snacks and beverages. Table seating.

☎ Railfone public telephone service available between New York and Washington, D.C.

Ⓢ Smoking is not permitted on this train.

Note: Service is financed in part through funds made available by the State Department of Transportation. State supported trains are operated at the discretion of each state and their operation is dependent upon continued state financial support.

AMTRAK
THERE'S SOMETHING ABOUT A TRAIN THAT'S MAGIC.

Source: Reprinted with permission from AMTRAK. Schedules subject to change.

Students must decide how a graph should represent a given situation. Choosing appropriate scales is an important part of this activity. The answers given are sample responses.

Exercise 1

The *x*-axis represents 24 hours and the *y*-axis shows temperatures from 0°F to 90°F. The time of year is early fall, so temperatures might range from 50°F to 80°F.

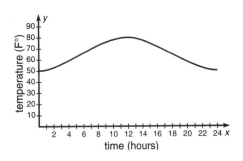

Exercise 2

The *x*-axis shows hours, and the *y*-axis shows inches. A 6-inch candle takes 2 hours and 15 minutes to burn down. The candle burns at a steady rate, so the graph is a straight line segment.

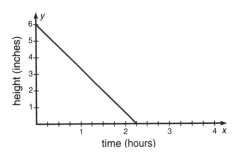

Exercise 3

The *x*-axis shows 80 years, and the *y*-axis shows heights up to 72 inches. The person described reached his full height by age 18 and shrank slightly after age 70.

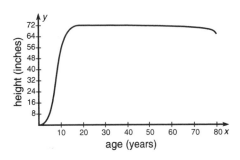

Exercise 4

The *x*-axis shows years, and the *y*-axis shows numbers of leaves. The number of leaves on the lilac bush varies from 30 to 2000.

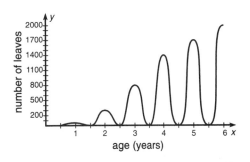

Draw a graph that matches each situation. Give a scale for each axis and write a few sentences explaining your choice of scale.

1. The temperature rose during the day and then fell as night approached. Show the temperature as a function of time.

2. A candle burned all the way down. Show the candle length as a function of time.

3. A child is born and grows old. Show this person's height as a function of time.

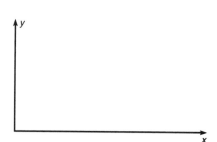

4. The number of leaves on a lilac bush changes from season to season and year to year. Show the number of leaves on the bush as a function of time.

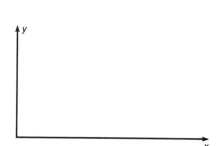

EXPLORING FORMULAS AND WORKING WITH DATA

Chapter 3 concentrates on applications. Lesson 3.1 has the format of the lessons in Chapter 1, but each exercise refers to an experiment that could be conducted in the classroom. Lesson 3.2 deals with the concept of density and Lesson 3.3 with Newton's Second Law. These lessons should serve as examples. If your class is studying a new concept or formula, a lesson similar to one of these can be designed to enhance students' understanding. The remaining lessons of this chapter include a series of experiments in which the students collect data or are given data to be analyzed. A TI-82 graphing calculator is suggested for lessons beginning with Lesson 3.4, and students will need facility with creating tables, drawing graphs of various types, and so on. A CBL (a hand-held calculator-based laboratory for data collection) was used to produce the data in Lessons 3.7 and 3.8.

LESSON 3.1   TEACHER NOTES

The three situations in this lesson all refer to experiments students may see in a science or math class. Students will need to think about each experiment to identify the correct graph.

Exercise 1

Graph **b**; it is the only one in which the time for a pendulum swing increases as the pendulum length increases as given in the statement. Graph **a** resembles the swing of a pendulum, but the time does not decrease and then increase as the pendulum length increases. Graph **c** is incorrect, as again the time varies up and down with the pendulum length. Graph **d** shows that the time decreases as the pendulum length increases, contrary to the statement given.

Exercise 2

Graph **a** matches the Superball™, as the bounces are rather high. Graph **b** matches the beanbag, as the beanbag does not bounce at all. Graph **c** matches the bowling ball, as a bowling ball bounces very little. Graph **d** matches the tennis ball, as a tennis ball bounces moderately, compared with the Superball™.

Exercise 3

Graph **a**; the spring clearly goes up and down. Graph **b** shows an up-and-down motion, but indicates that a force is applied to the object. Graph **c** shows that the object does not move up and down at all, and graph **d** indicates that the object rises once and then drops.

1. The time it takes for a full swing of a pendulum increases as the length of the pendulum increases. Which graph below best describes this situation? Explain why you chose that graph and why the other graphs do not describe the situation.

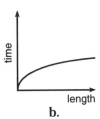

a.

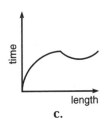

b.

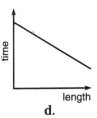

c.

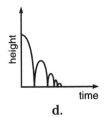

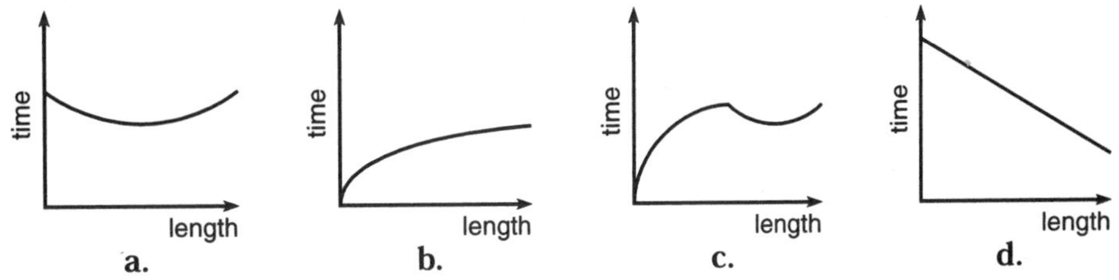

2. A Superball™, a tennis ball, a bowling ball, and a beanbag are dropped from the same height. Match one of the graphs below to each object. Explain your choices.

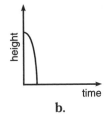

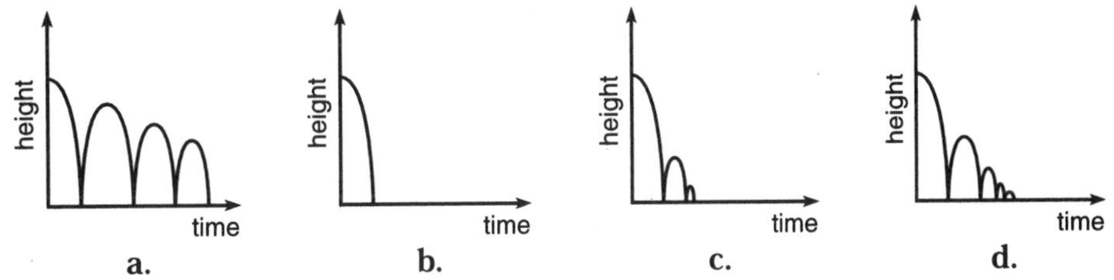

a.

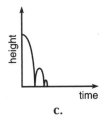

b.

c.

d.

3. A weight attached to a spring is moving up and down. Which graph below best describes this situation? Explain why you chose that graph and why the other graphs do not describe the situation.

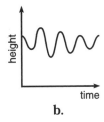

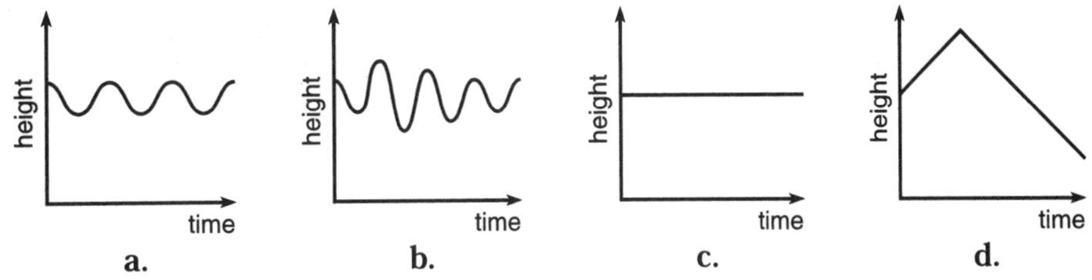

a.

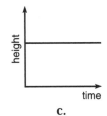

b.

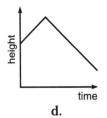

c.

d.

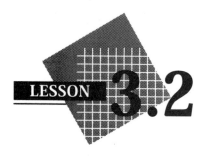

TEACHER NOTES

This lesson is good if your class is studying density in science. Once again, students differentiate between the graphs of constant, increasing, and decreasing functions. For Exercise 4, students need to recall the definition of slope. For Exercises 1–3, you might discuss with students why the incorrect graphs do not describe the given situation.

Exercise 1

Graph **b**; it indicates that no matter how much matter is present, its density is the same.

Exercise 2

Graph **a**; it indicates that the more mass (or weight) that can be contained in 1 cubic centimeter, the more dense the substance is.

Exercise 3

Graph **c**; it indicates that as more volume is needed to contain the same mass (or weight), the less dense the substance is.

Exercise 4

In each case, the slope indicates the density of the substance. Students may be asked to find the density of each substance. The density of water is 1 gram per cubic centimeter (g/cc); the density of oak is 0.6 g/cc; the density of iodine is 4.9 g/cc; the density of aluminum is 2.7 g/cc). Each density is calculated by dividing the y-coordinate by the x-coordinate of the point indicated. (This represents the change in y over the change in x where the two chosen points are the point indicated and $(0, 0)$.)

Exercise 5

Yes; oak will float in water.

For each set of graphs, choose the one that best matches the situation. Write a sentence explaining your choice.

1. The *density* of a substance refers to the quantity of matter in a unit of volume. Density is expressed as the quotient of mass (or weight) divided by volume. One pound of lead has the same density as 10 pounds of lead. One ounce of cork has the same density as 6 ounces of cork. Even if the amount of a particular substance increases, its density remains the same.

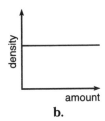 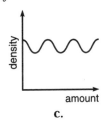 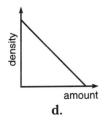 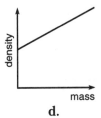

   a. b. c. d.

2. The greater the mass (or weight) of matter in the same unit of volume, the *more* dense the matter is.

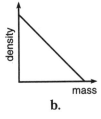 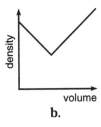 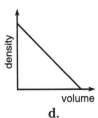 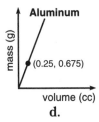

   a. b. c. d.

3. The greater the volume needed to contain the same mass (or weight) of matter, the *less* dense the matter is.

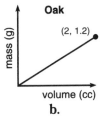 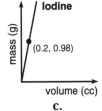

   a. b. c. d.

4. For each substance listed, volume in cubic centimeters is graphed along the *x*-axis (horizontal axis) and mass in grams is graphed along the *y*-axis (vertical axis). What is indicated by the slope of each line?

   Water (1, 1) **Oak** (2, 1.2) **Iodine** (0.2, 0.98) **Aluminum** (0.25, 0.675)

   a. b. c. d.

5. A substance will float in water if it is less dense than water and sink if it is more dense. Will any of the substances in Exercise 4 float in water?

TEACHER NOTES

This lesson explores direct and indirect variation using Newton's second law: *force = mass × acceleration.* In Exercises 1, 3, and 4, one of the variables in the formula is held constant and the relationship between the remaining two variables is pictured. Exercise 2 shows that the acceleration due to gravity is constant. In all of the exercises, you might discuss with students why the incorrect graphs do not describe the given situation.

Exercise 1

Graph **b**; the acceleration is constant and the force increases as the mass increases.

Exercise 2

Graph **a**; the acceleration due to gravity does not change as the mass increases.

Exercise 3

Graph **a**; the mass is constant and the force increases as the acceleration increases.

Exercise 4

Graph **c**; the force is constant and the acceleration decreases as the mass increases.

LESSON 3.3

For each set of graphs, choose the graph that best matches the situation. Write a sentence explaining why you made the particular choice you did. The exercises in this lesson explore Newton's second law: ***force* = *mass* × *acceleration*.**

1. Any change in motion is an acceleration. A force is needed to obtain an acceleration. The greater the mass, the greater the force required to produce a given acceleration.

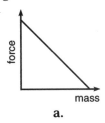
a.

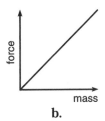
b.

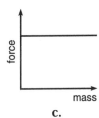
c.

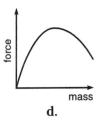
d.

2. Gravity is the force of attraction between any two masses. In particular, we mean the attraction of the earth for small objects near its surface. The force of gravity causes objects to accelerate. In this case, the acceleration of any object, regardless of its mass, is the same. So as mass increases, the acceleration due to gravity remains constant.

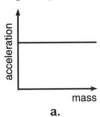
a.

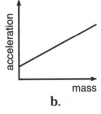
b.

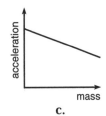
c.

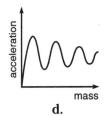
d.

3. For a particular mass, the greater the acceleration desired, the greater the force required.

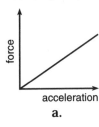
a.

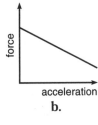
b.

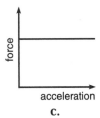
c.

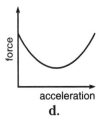
d.

4. For a given force, the greater the mass, the less the acceleration produced.

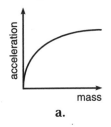
a.

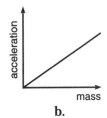
b.

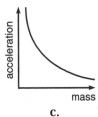
c.

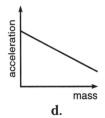
d.

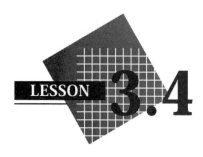

If you wish, you may have students complete this lesson using graphing calculators. For this experiment, divide the class into groups of three. Each group will need a container with around 300 **m&ms**® in it, a tray for the **m&ms**, and a second container to hold the **m&ms** that are removed after each spill. Students may eat the **m&ms** that are removed after each of the 10 trials. First have the students count the **m&ms** in their containers and record the results. Then have the students gently spill the **m&ms** onto the tray, remove the ones with an **m** showing, and record the number of **m&ms** left on the tray. This step is repeated 9 times.

Exercise 4

Students' scatter plots will vary.

Exercise 5

The curve corresponding to the cooling of a hot piece of aluminum foil

Exercise 6

For the point (5, 18), a possible statement is, "After spilling the **m&ms** 5 times and removing all **m&ms** with the **m** showing after each spill, 18 **m&ms** were left."

Exercise 7

One might expect the points to fit the curve $y = A\left(\frac{1}{2}\right)^x$ where A is the initial number of **m&ms**. Approximately half of the **m&ms** should remain after each spill, since there is a 50-50 chance that an **m** will appear on top of each **m&m** when the **m&ms** are spilled.

If students have used a graphing calculator, have them enter their data and draw a scatter plot. Sample data are illustrated here.

L1	L2	L3
0	297	-----
1	177	
2	96	
3	57	
4	31	
5	18	
6	14	

L1 (1) = 0

L1	L2	L3
5	18	
6	14	
7	11	
8	7	
9	7	
10	3	

L1 (12) =

Students can use the [TRACE] feature to locate a point for Exercise 6. Have them actually plot the curve $y = A\left(\frac{1}{2}\right)^x$ to see if the curve is similar to that of the scatter plot. The curve for the data above is given here.

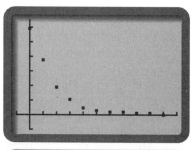

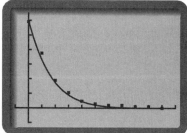

This lesson involves an experiment in which you will collect data and try to fit a curve to the data. You need a container of **m&m**®s, a tray, and an empty container.

1. Count the **m&m**s in your bucket. This number corresponds to $x = 0$, the number of **m&m**s after 0 trials or spills. Enter this number in the y column, across from 0.

2. Gently spill the **m&m**s onto your tray, and remove all that have the **m** showing. Count the **m&m**s that remain, and enter this number in the table for trial 1.

3. Repeat this procedure 9 times. After each trial, record the number of remaining **m&m**s next to the number of that trial.

x (trial number)	y (**m&m**s)
0	
1	
2	
3	
4	
5	
6	
7	
8	
9	
10	

4. Plot the data on the grid at the right. You now have a *scatter plot* of the data.

5. What type of curve does the scatter plot suggest? Are you reminded of the curve corresponding to a cooling of a hot piece of aluminum foil or to the amount of gas left in a tank after x hours of driving?

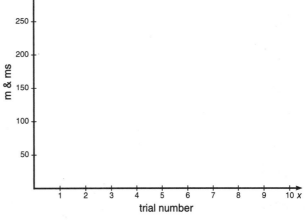

6. Choose the coordinates of one of the points, and write a statement about the experiment using the information obtained from that point.

7. How many **m&m**s did you start with? About how many would you expect after the first spill and removal? Each time you spilled the **m&m**s, how many did you expect to remove? Try to think of a curve you would expect the data points to fit. Explain your reasoning.

Exercise 1

A partial listing of the data is given.

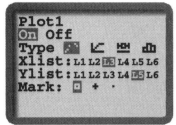

L₃	L₄	L₅
0	16000	15350
1	13200	14050
2	10575	12800
3	9450	11825
4	7450	10225
5	6125	8850
6	5100	7525

L3(1)=0

Exercise 2

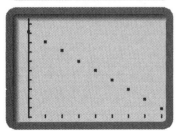

Plot1
On Off
Type: ▪ ∠ ᴴᴴ ᕧ
Xlist: L1 L2 **L3** L4 L5 L6
Ylist: L1 L2 L3 L4 **L5** L6
Mark: ▫ + ·

Exercise 3

A straight line

Exercise 4

For the point (1992, 11,825), a possible statement is, "The suggested price for a 1992 Honda is $11,825."

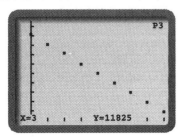

X=3   Y=11825

Exercise 5

The line obtained using the median-median approach and the line obtained using residuals are given in Exercise 8. At this point, students can try their own methods and explain their reasoning. They may try to fit several lines to the data by experimentation. One approach is to look at the slopes of the lines joining adjacent points and come up with a slope for the guess by taking the average, as shown here.

L₄	L₅	L₆
1300	15350	14050
1250	14050	12800
975	12800	11825
1600	11825	10225
1375	10225	8850
1325	8850	7525
1250	7525	6275

L4(1)=1300

1-Var Stats
x̄=1296.428571
Σx=9075
Σx²=11971875
Sx=185.6455917
σx=171.8744202
↓n=7

L5 was copied to L6 in one step; the first entry was deleted and a zero added to the end of the list. L4 was formed by subtracting L6 from L5 in one step. To find the average, one-variable stats were performed on L4 after deleting its final entry. The line was then approximated to be $y = -1296x + 15{,}350$. (We used (0, 15,350) to get the y-intercept.)

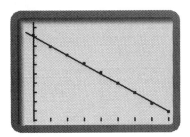

Exercise 6

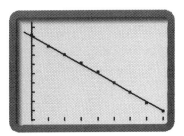

Exercise 7

The fact that the numbers differ in **L4** indicates that it is impossible to get an exact fit.

Exercise 8

The regression equations are given below. All three lines—these two and the one obtained in Exercise 5—appear to fit the data very closely.

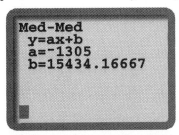

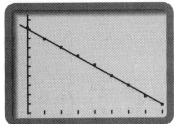

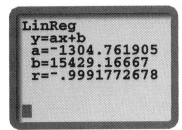

Exercise 9

The solutions for the Taurus follow the same format as those for the Accord.

2.

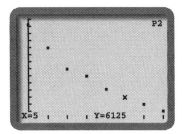

3. The points in the scatter plot appear to lie along a straight line, although this is not as evident as with the Accord.

4. For the point (1990, 6,125), a possible statement is, "The suggested price for a 1990 Taurus is $6125."

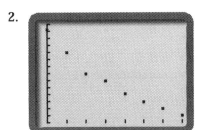

5. See Exercise 5 for the Honda Accord.

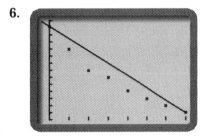

L1 (1) = 16000

L1	L2	L3
16000	13200	2800
13200	10575	2625
10575	9450	1125
9450	7450	2000
7450	6125	1325
6125	5100	1025
5100	4000	1100

1-Var Stats
x̄=1714.285714
Σx=12000
Σx²=24012500
Sx=757.3056878
σx=701.1288274
↓n=7

L1 was copied to L2 in one step; the first entry was deleted and a zero added to the end of the list. L3 was formed by subtracting L2 from L1 in one step. To find the average, one-variable stats were performed on L3 after deleting its final entry. The line was then approximated to be $y = -1714x + 16{,}000$. (We use the data point $(0, 16{,}000)$ to get the y-intercept.)

6.

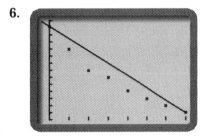

7. The fact that the numbers differ in L3 indicates that it is impossible to get an exact fit.

8. The regression equations are given below. These lines clearly fit better than the one in Exercise 5.

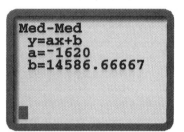

Med-Med
y=ax+b
a=⁻1620
b=14586.66667

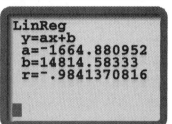

LinReg
y=ax+b
a=⁻1664.880952
b=14814.58333
r=⁻.9841370816

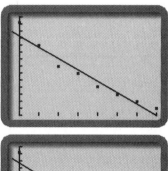

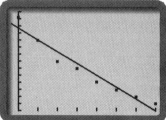

Exercise   10

Answers will vary.

The 1995 National Automobile Dealers Association *(N.A.D.A.) Official Used Car Guide* gives dealers suggested retail prices for used cars. The data below were taken from the guide. The date indicates the model year of the used car, and the price is for a standard sedan that has not been driven to excess.

Year	Ford Taurus 4-door Sedan GL	Honda Accord 4-door Sedan Dx
1995	$16,000	$15,350
1994	13,200	14,050
1993	10,575	12,800
1992	9,450	11,825
1991	7,450	10,225
1990	6,125	8,850
1989	5,100	7,525
1988	4,000	6,275

Source: *N.A.D.A. Used Car Guide, 1995*

1. Enter all the data in three separate lists into your graphing calculator. You may choose to enter 0 for 1995, 1 for 1994, and so on, to indicate the age of the used car.

2. Draw a scatter plot of the year (or age) versus the price for the Honda Accord.

3. What type of curve does the scatter plot suggest?

4. Use TRACE to locate a point and write a statement about the price using the information obtained from the point.

5. Try to think of a curve you would expect the data points to fit. Explain your reasoning.

6. Plot this curve to see if your conjecture is correct.

7. Is it possible to get an exact fit?

8. Try using the appropriate built-in regression equation(s). Record the result.

9. Repeat Exercises 2–8 using the data for the Taurus sedan.

10. Which car do you feel is a better buy? Explain your reasoning.

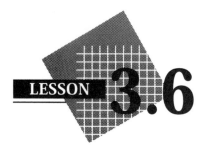

TEACHER NOTES

Exercise 1

For the line whose first entry is 70, a possible statement is, "After 1 minute 10 seconds, the temperature of the foil is approximately 96.93°F."

Exercise 2

Since 104°F = 40°C, we see from the table that the foil's temperature was 104° between 40 and 45 seconds.

Exercise 3

As time went by, the foil cooled more and more slowly. You can tell this from both the graph and the table. The numbers in **L4** decrease more and more slowly down the list, and the graph is almost horizontal after $2\frac{1}{2}$ minutes.

Exercise 4

After 1 minute 40 seconds, the temperature of the foil was 91.62°F.

Exercise 5

The curve is exponential in shape, so we expect the model to be exponential with k negative. When $t = 0$, we put 0 into the model and correctly get the initial temperature of the foil. We know objects cool to the temperature of the room they are in, and the model likewise is close to the temperature of the room when t is large.

Exercise 6

According to the model, the graphing calculator gave the foil's initial temperature as approximately 127.75°F. The actual temperature of the foil after 1 minute 40 seconds was 91.62°F, as stated in Exercise 4.

LESSON 3.6

A hair dryer was used to heat a piece of aluminum foil covering a temperature probe. Temperature readings were then taken every 5 seconds for 3 minutes and recorded in the lists shown below. The list L3 shows the number of seconds. The list L4 shows the corresponding temperature in degrees Celsius (°C). A graph of the data is on the next page. The temperatures are given in degrees Celsius (°C).

L3	L4	L5
5	48.39	————
10	47.23	
15	46.02	
20	44.77	
25	43.67	
30	42.71	
35	41.64	

L5=

L3	L4	L5
40	40.51	
45	39.66	
50	38.78	
55	37.98	
60	37.3	
65	36.63	
70	36.07	

L3(14)=70

L3	L4	L5
75	35.51	
80	34.96	
85	34.32	
90	33.97	
95	33.44	
100	33.12	
105	32.79	

L3(21)=105

L3	L4	L5
110	32.46	
115	32.13	
120	31.81	
125	31.59	
130	31.37	
135	31.07	
140	30.94	

L3(28)=140

L3	L4	L5
145	30.64	
150	30.53	
155	30.32	
160	30.21	
165	30.1	
170	29.99	
175	29.88	

L3(35)=175

1. Choose a line in one of the tables and use the given information to write a statement about the foil. Convert degrees Celsius (°C) to degrees Fahrenheit (°F) using the formula $F = 1.8C + 32$. Also change seconds to minutes, if appropriate.

2. When was the temperature of the foil 104° F? Use the formula $C = \frac{F-32}{1.8}$.

3. What do you notice about the rate of change? As time goes by, did the foil cool more quickly or more slowly? Can you tell this from the graph, from the table, or from both? Explain your answer.

4. Look at Figure 1. A point is indicated. Use the given information to write a sentence about the foil. Again convert to °F and minutes.

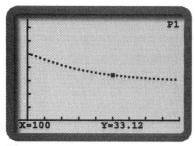

Figure 1

5. The mathematical model for a cooling curve is $T = A(e^{kt}) + C$, where C is the temperature of the room and A is the difference between the temperature of the room and the initial temperature of the object being cooled. k depends on the object and the container in which it is being cooled. Try to explain why this is a good model. Is k positive or negative? When $t = 0$, what is T?

6. The graphing calculator can be used to find a curve to fit the data. The equation and the graph for this curve are Figures 2 and 3. According to this model, what was the initial temperature of the foil? What was the actual temperature of the foil after 1 minute 40 seconds?

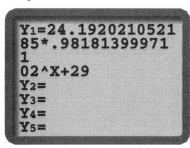

Figure 2

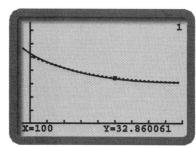

Figure 3

LESSON 3.7   TEACHER NOTES

This lesson was designed for use with a TI-82 overhead calculator and a CBL unit.

Exercise 1

The data in graph **a** are produced as someone stands 18 feet away from the motion detector and walks toward the detector at a steady pace of 3 feet per second. An approximation for graph **b** is produced as someone starts 9 feet away from the detector, walks back to 14 feet, and then walks forward to 4 feet within the space of $1\frac{1}{2}$ seconds. The person walks back and forth again in about 2 seconds. The person then repeats the cycle another time and then walks back to 9 feet away. For graph **c**, a person walks from 18 feet away to 9 feet away in two seconds, stands still for 2 seconds, and then walks up to the detector in 2 seconds.

Exercise 2

Data for horizontal lines are produced as someone stands still. This makes sense in terms of distance and time. To produce a horizontal line, distance from the detector must not change as time goes by. For graph **a**, the person stands 2 feet away, for graph **b** 12 feet away, and for graph **c** 18 feet away.

Exercise 3

These data are all produced as someone walks at a steady pace away from the detector. The steeper the slope desired, the faster the person must walk. This makes sense in terms of time and distance, as a steeper line indicates more distance is covered in less time.

1. Try to reproduce the data pictured in the graphs below as you walk in front of a motion detector.

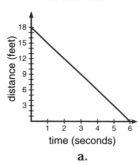

a.

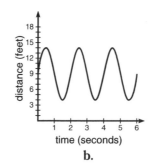

b.

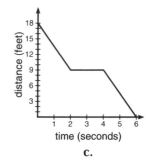

c.

2. Now try to reproduce the data pictured in the graphs below. Explain how to produce data for a horizontal line. Why does this make sense in terms of distance and time?

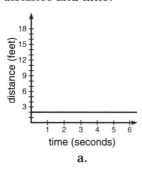

a.

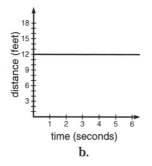

b.

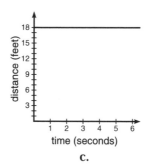

c.

3. Try to reproduce the data shown in the three graphs below. Explain how to produce data for a line with a steeper slope. Why does this make sense in terms of distance and time?

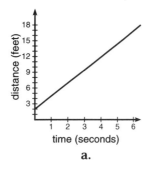

a.

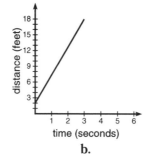

b.

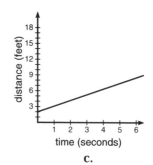

c.

TEACHER NOTES

This experiment can be tried with a CBL unit. If the lesson is done before a classroom demonstration, it will help students understand what to expect and how to interpret the tables. Have them round their answers to the nearest thousandth.

Exercise 1

For the line whose first entry is 0.06, a possible statement is, "After 0.06 second, the height of the soccer ball was about 4.566 feet, and it was falling at about 5.042 feet per second."

Exercise 2

The height was 2 feet between 0.32 and 0.34 seconds. Some students may answer that the height was never 2 feet since the reading does not occur in the table.

Exercise 3

Subtracting adjacent entries in **L4** gives the change in height that occurs between two readings. The time interval between readings is 0.02 of a second. The quotient, change in height divided by change in time, gives us average velocity. The average velocity goes from 3.421 to 13.5 feet per second during the fall. The negative sign indicates the object is falling.

Exercise 4

A possible statement is, "After 0.18 second, the height of the soccer ball is about 3.749 feet."

Exercise 5

According to the model, the soccer ball was 4.807 feet above the ground for the reading taken at $t = 0$. The actual reading is 4.8002. When an object is thrown into the air, theoretically its path is modeled by the formula $h = -16t^2 + v_0 t + c$, where h is the the height at time t, c is the initial height, and v_0 the initial velocity. The equation given by the calculator indicates the ball's initial velocity was 3.05. The recorded value was 3.421.

A deflated soccer ball was dropped from a height of 5 feet onto a protected motion detector. Readings were taken every 0.02 of a second and the height was recorded. A portion of the data was selected using the CBL program "select." These data appear in the three lists below. A graph of the data is shown below the lists.

The height is given in feet. The list L5 was formed by subtracting adjacent entries in list L4 and dividing by 0.02, thus creating a list that gives the average velocity for each time interval.

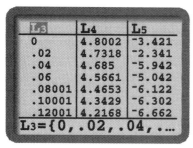

L3	L4	L5
0	4.8002	‾3.421
.02	4.7318	‾2.341
.04	4.685	‾5.942
.06	4.5661	‾5.042
.08001	4.4653	‾6.122
.10001	4.3429	‾6.302
.12001	4.2168	‾6.662

L3={0,.02,.04,...

L3	L4	L5
.14001	4.0836	‾7.923
.16002	3.9252	‾8.823
.18002	3.7487	‾8.283
.20002	3.5831	‾9.723
.22002	3.3886	‾10.08
.24001	3.1869	‾9.723
.26002	2.9925	‾11.88

L3(14)=.260023

1. Choose a line in the table and use that information to write a statement about the fall of the soccer ball.

2. When was the height 2 feet?

3. Explain why **L5** gives the average velocity for a time interval of 0.02 second. Write a statement about the average velocity.

4. Look below on the left at the graph of the data. Use the point indicated to write a statement about the soccer ball.

5. The path of a dropped object is modeled by a quadratic function. The graphing calculator can be used to find a quadratic curve and equation to fit the data. The equation is shown below on the right. According to this model, what was the height at time $t = 0$, which corresponds to the first point selected? What does the table indicate for $t = 0$?

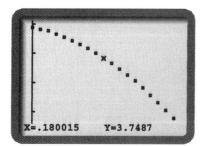

X=.180015   Y=3.7487

QuadReg
y=ax²+bx+c
a=‾15.36104267
b=‾3.050228071
c=4.806901893

CONCENTRATING ON ALGEBRA

In this chapter, students explore traditional topics through visual exercises. Many of the activities assume the use of a graphing calculator, but can also be completed with paper and pencil. The materials include several exercises designed to assist students in finding a correct equation for a given situation. The lessons in which students create and use a table, an equation, and a graph to describe a situation are very important; these lessons should be thoroughly understood by all algebra students.

LESSON 4.1 TEACHER NOTES

The Pythagorean theorem is used to prove the Distance Formula and is, of course, one of the great theorems in the field of mathematics. It is assumed that students have not had a formal course in geometry but have a basic middle-school understanding of area and angles.

Exercise 1

$a + b$ and $a + b$

Exercise 2

$(a + b)(a + b) = a^2 + 2ab + b^2$

Exercise 3

$\frac{1}{2}ab$

Exercise 4

c and c; $c \times c$, or c^2

Exercise 5

$4\left(\frac{1}{2}\right)ab + c^2 = 2ab + c^2$

Exercise 6

$a^2 + 2ab + b^2 = 2ab + c^2$, or $a^2 + b^2 = c^2$

Make sure students understand that they have given a proof of the Pythagorean theorem: In a right triangle, the square of the hypotenuse is equal to the sum of the squares of the other two sides.

1. The large square above is made up of four identical right triangles and a smaller square. What are the dimensions of the large square?

2. Give the area of the square in terms of these dimensions. Expand this expression.

3. Give an expression for the area of each triangle.

4. What are the dimensions of the smaller square? What is its area?

5. Now give an expression for the area of the large square using the fact that it is the sum of the areas of four triangles and a square.

6. Equate the two expressions you wrote in Exercises 2 and 5 and simplify.

TEACHER NOTES

Exercise 1

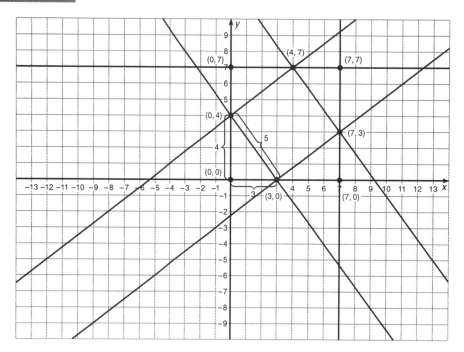

Exercise 2

See graph for coordinates.

Exercise 3

Lengths of sides: 3 and 4; length of hypotenuse: 5

Exercise 4

Smaller square: 25 square units; triangle: 6 square units

Exercise 5

Area of large square: $7 \times 7 = 49$ square units; sum of the areas of triangles and small square: $4(6) + 25 = 49$ square units

Extension

As an extension, have students try to make a figure similar to the one above that uses the line $y = -\frac{3}{2}x + 3$. Students can first graph that line and then use the triangle it creates with the axes as one of the four triangles of the large square. They can determine the points needed to complete the figure, find the equations of the lines that pass through the points, and repeat Exercises 3–5.

1. On the grid below, let each grid mark along the *x*- and *y*-axes represent 1 unit.

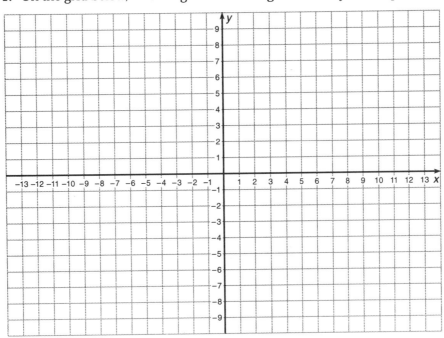

Graph the following lines.

$$y=0 \qquad x=0 \qquad y=-\tfrac{4}{3}+4 \qquad y=\tfrac{3}{4}x+4$$

$$y=7 \qquad x=7 \qquad y=-\tfrac{4}{3}x+\tfrac{37}{3} \qquad y=\tfrac{3}{4}x+\left(-\tfrac{9}{4}\right)$$

2. You should recognize in the upper-right quadrant a figure similar to the one you used in Lesson 4.1 to prove the Pythagorean theorem. Indicate the coordinates of each corner of every square.

3. Find the length of each side of each right triangle, and then use the Pythagorean theorem to find the length of each hypotenuse.

4. Find the area of the smaller square and the area of each right triangle.

5. Use the dimensions to calculate the area of the large square. What would be another way to calculate the area of the large square? Does this lead to the same result?

TEACHER NOTES

In this lesson, students derive the Distance Formula and the formula for the midpoint of a line segment. These are standard topics studied in algebra. You may need to review the concept of absolute value with your students.

Exercise 1

Sample points are given.

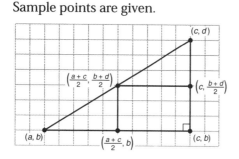

Exercise 2

(a, b); see graph.

Exercise 3

$|c - a|$

Exercise 4

$|b - d|$

Exercise 5

[Distance between (a, b) and (c, d)]^2
$= (c - a)^2 + (b - d)^2$, so
[distance between (a, b) and (c, d)]
$= \sqrt{(c-a)^2+(b-d)^2}$.

Exercise 6

$\left(c, b+\dfrac{d-b}{2}\right)$ or $\left(c, \dfrac{b+d}{2}\right)$

Exercise 7

$\left(a+\dfrac{c-a}{2}, b\right)$ or $\left(\dfrac{c+a}{2}, b\right)$

Exercise 8

$\left(\dfrac{c+a}{2}, \dfrac{b+d}{2}\right)$; this is the midpoint because the triangles are congruent and the sides of congruent triangles have the same measure.

Extension

As an extension, you might have students plot two specific points (a, b) and (c, d) on a four-quadrant grid. Have students give the numerical coordinates for their points and verify the formula. This can be done first with points in the same quadrant and then with points in different quadrants.

1. Mark any two points (*a*, *b*) and (*c*, *d*) on the grid below. Notice that the axes and scales are not given. With a ruler, draw the line segment joining the two points, and draw the lines *y* = *b* and *x* = *c*.

2. Give the coordinates of the point of intersection of the vertical and horizontal lines in Exercise 1. Indicate this point on the graph. Note that a right triangle has been formed with your line segment as the hypotenuse. Mark the coordinates of the right angle, and outline the triangle.

3. Find the distance between (*a*, *b*) and the point of intersection you found. Indicate the distance on your graph.

4. Find the distance between (*c*, *d*) and the point of intersection. Indicate the distance on your graph.

5. Now use the Pythagorean theorem to find the distance between (*a*, *b*) and (*c*, *d*).

6. Find the point halfway between (*c*, *d*) and the point of intersection. Plot the point on the graph.

7. Find the point halfway between (*a*, *b*) and the point of intersection. Plot the point on the graph.

8. Complete the rectangle formed with the two points from Exercises 6 and 7 and the point (*c*, *b*). Find the coordinates for the fourth corner. Try to explain why the point at the fourth corner is the midpoint of the line segment joining (*a*, *b*) and (*c*, *d*).

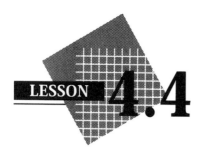

TEACHER NOTES

This lesson is designed to help students understand the equation for the slope of a line and gain some insight into why that equation is valid.

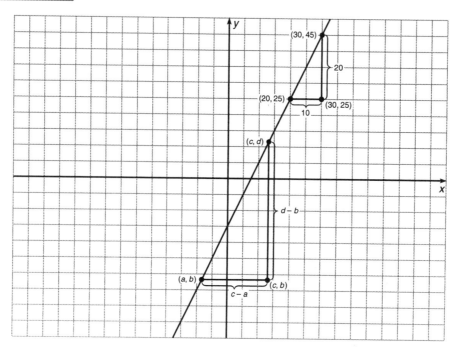

$$\frac{d-b}{c-a} = \frac{20}{10} = 2$$

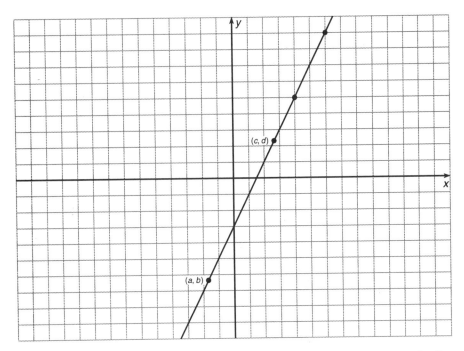

The line with equation $y = 2x - 15$ is graphed above. Four points on the line are indicated.

1. Consider the points (a, b) and (c, d). Draw the lines for $y = b$ and $x = c$.

2. Give the algebraic expression for the coordinates of the point of intersection of the lines for $y = b$ and $x = c$. Mark the coordinates for this point on the graph.

3. Give the algebraic expression for the distance between (a, b) and the point of intersection you marked. Indicate the distance on your graph.

4. Give the algebraic expression for distance between (c, d) and this point of intersection. Indicate the distance on your graph.

5. Let each grid mark along both axes represent 5 units. Find the coordinates for the other two points.

6. Follow the steps outlined in Exercises 1–4, drawing the appropriate vertical and horizontal lines. This time, give numerical coordinates and distances.

7. Two similar right triangles have been formed, so the sides are proportional. Give the ratio of vertical leg to horizontal leg for each of the triangles. Equate the two expressions to get the equation for the slope of the line.

TEACHER NOTES

The exercises in this lesson and the next are designed to help students understand the condition under which two lines are perpendicular and gain some insight into why that condition guarantees the two lines will be perpendicular.

Exercise 1

The coordinates of points A and B are shown on the graph.

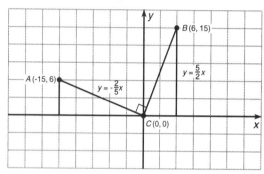

Exercise 2

Slope of line $AC = -\frac{2}{5}$; slope of line $BC = \frac{5}{2}$

Exercise 3

Since the triangles are congruent right triangles, we can substitute the measure of the smaller angle of one for the measure of the smaller angle of the other; so the sum of the two acute angles at $(0, 0)$ is 90°. Since the angle here is a straight angle that measures 180°, the measure of the angle between the two triangles' angles is 90° and the angle is a right angle.

Exercise 4

The slopes of the lines are negative reciprocals; that is, their product is -1.

Exercise 5

No; the slopes would not be different as the ratio $\dfrac{\text{change in } y}{\text{change in } x}$ would remain the same.

Exercise 6

The slopes would now be different as the ratio $\dfrac{\text{change in } y}{\text{change in } x}$ would not be the same. When the scales along the axes are different, lines that are perpendicular will no longer appear perpendicular, and lines that appear perpendicular may not be.

LESSON 4.5

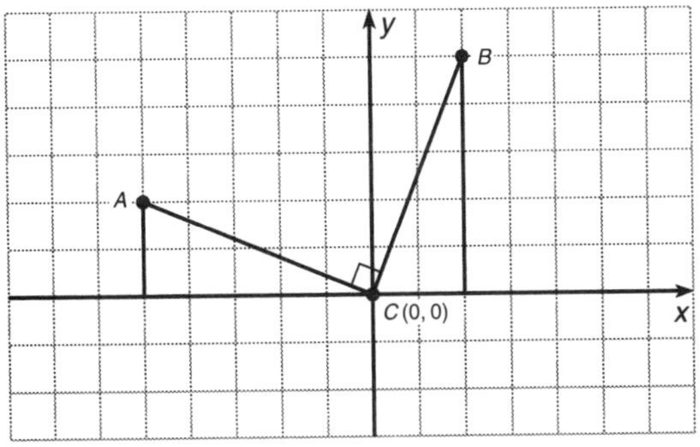

In the graph above, each grid mark along both axes represents 3 units.

1. What are the coordinates of points *A* and *B?*

2. Find the slope for the line passing through points *A* and *C* and the slope for the line passing through points *B* and *C*.

3. By considering the angles of the triangles pictured, explain how you know the two lines are perpendicular.

4. What do you notice about the slopes of the two lines?

5. Would the slopes be different if each grid mark represented 5 units rather than 3 units?

6. Would the slopes be different if the grid marks along the *x*-axis represented 3 units and those along the *y*-axis represented 5 units?

Exercises 1–2

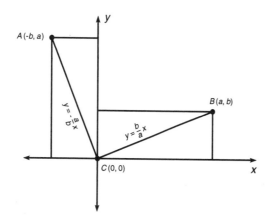

Exercise 3

Since the triangles are congruent right triangles, we can substitute the measure of the smaller angle of one for the measure of the smaller angle of the other; so the sum of the two acute angles at (0, 0) is 90°. Since the angle here is a straight angle that measures 180°, the measure of the angle between the two triangles' angles is 90° and the angle is a right angle.

Exercise 4

The slopes are negative reciprocals; that is, their product is -1.

LESSON 4.6

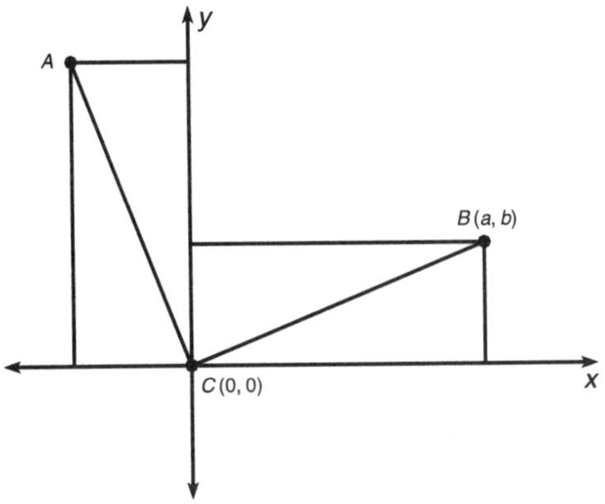

1. In the graph above, there are 4 congruent right triangles, and the scales along the x- and y-axes are the same. Use the coordinates of point B to help you find the coordinates of point A.

2. Find the slope for the line passing through points A and C and the slope for the line passing through points B and C.

3. By considering the angles of the triangles pictured, explain how you know the two lines are perpendicular.

4. What do you notice about the slopes of the two lines?

TEACHER NOTES

This exercise is fun for students to do and gives them practice writing an equation for a line given a graph of the line. You will probably have to review with students the slope-intercept form for the equation of a line. For each graph, you may ask the following questions:

- How many equations are you looking for?
- Are any of the lines parallel? If so, what will be true of the equations of these lines?
- How many lines have positive slopes and how many have negative slopes? Do any have zero slope?
- What are the y-intercepts of the lines?
- Give the slopes of the lines.

Exercise 1

```
Y₁ = -2X
Y₂ = 3-2X
Y₃ = 1+2X
Y₄ = 3+2X
Y₅ =
Y₆ =
Y₇ =
Y₈ =
```

Exercise 2

```
Y₁ = 1
Y₂ = 2-X
Y₃ = 2+X
Y₄ = -1
Y₅ = -2-X
Y₆ = -2+x
Y₇ =
Y₈ =
```

Exercise 3

Answers will vary. You may want to have students share their equations and graphs with the class.

The screens in Exercises 1 and 2 are the result of pressing ZOOM 4 on a TI-82 calculator. On your own graphing calculator, try to reproduce the design. Then record the equations you used.

1.

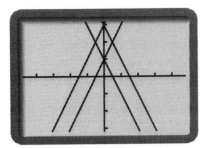

2.

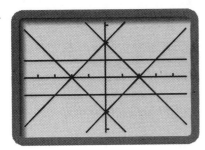

3. Make up your own linear design on the graph below. Record your equations. Give the equations to a friend and see if he or she can reproduce your design using your equations.

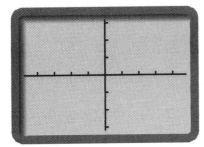

TEACHER NOTES

This lesson should help students understand the effect of increasing and decreasing the magnitude of the slope of a line. It also points out the effect of scale on the appearance of the line.

Exercise 1

```
Y₁=X+4
Y₂=X-4
Y₃=-X+4
Y₄=-X-4
Y₅=
Y₆=
Y₇=
Y₈=
```

Exercise 2

The lines rise and fall more steeply than their counterparts in Exercise 1. The y-intercepts are unaffected because substituting $x = 0$ into the equations yields the same result as before. The x-intercepts are half those in Exericse 1, as can be seen by substituting $y = 0$ into each new equation and solving for x.

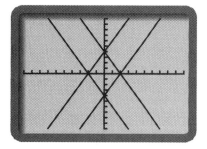

Exercise 3

The lines rise and fall more gently than their counterparts in Exercise 1. The y-intercepts are unaffected, as substituting $x = 0$ into the equations yields the same result as before. The x-intercepts are double those in Exercise 1, as can be seen by substituting $y = 0$ into each new equation and solving for x.

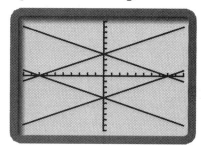

Exercise 4

```
WINDOW FORMAT
Xmin=-20
 Xmax=20
 Xscl=2
 Ymin=-10
 Ymax=10
 Yscl=1
```

1. The screen below is the result of pressing ZOOM 6 on a TI-82 calculator. On your own graphing calculator, try to reproduce the design. Then record the equations you used.

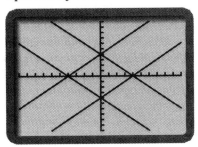

2. What is the effect of doubling the slope in each equation in Exercise 1? Describe the effect in words. How are the lines different? Are the *y*-intercepts different? Are the *x*-intercepts different? Carefully draw the design on the grid below.

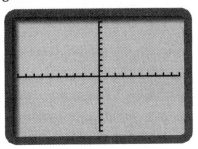

3. What is the effect of dividing by 2 the slopes in each equation in Exercise 1? Describe the effect in words. How are the lines different? Are the *y*-intercepts different? Are about the *x*-intercepts different? Carefully draw the design on the grid below.

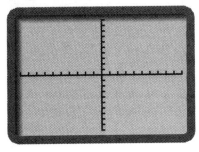

4. You can produce the design in Exercise 2 by using the equations from Exercise 1 and altering the window rather than the slopes. Find this window. The appearance of the graph is thus dependent on the window.

Exercise 1

$y = 0.5x$, $y = x$, $y = 2x$, $y = 4x$; the equations are easiest to find by looking at points on the lines with x-coordinate equal to 4 or 2.

Exercise 2

$y = -3x + 9$, $y = -3x + 6$, $y = -3x + 3$, $y = -3x$, $y = -3x - 3$, $y = -3x - 6$, $y = -3x - 9$; to graph these at the same time, you may use the following notation:

```
Y1 -3X-{9,6,3,0,
-3,-6,-9}
Y2=
Y3=
Y4=
Y5=
Y6=
Y7=
```

A corresponding equation can be used to graph the lines in Exercise 1 using a single equation. You may feel that this notation is not appropriate to use with your students.

Exercise 3

The lines fall at the same rate as their counterparts rise in Exercise 1. The lines all pass through the origin.

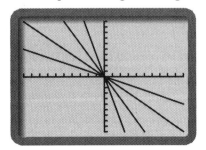

Exercise 4

The functions are all increasing rather than decreasing. The y-intercepts are unaffected, as substituting $x = 0$ into the equations yields the same result as before. Each x-intercept is the opposite of its counterpart, as can be seen by substituting $y = 0$ into each new equation and solving for x.

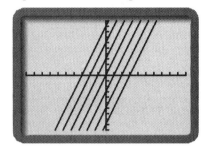

Exercise 5

$y = mx + b$ is increasing if m is positive and decreasing if m is negative.

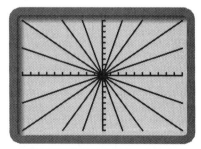

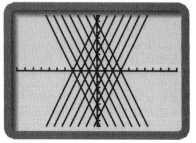

1. The screen at the right is the result of pressing ZOOM 6 on a TI-82 calculator. On your own graphing calculator, try to reproduce the design. Then record the equations you used. Each of the lines passes through the origin (0, 0) and is the graph of a linear function. In each case, decide if the function is increasing or decreasing.

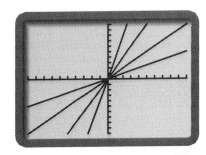

2. Repeat the steps in Exercise 1 with the following design. Note here, however, only one line passes through the origin.

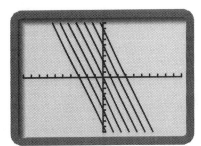

3. What is the effect of taking the opposite of the slope in each equation in Exercise 1? Describe the effect in words. How are the lines different? Are the *y*-intercepts different? Are the *x*-intercepts different? Carefully draw the design on the grid at the right.

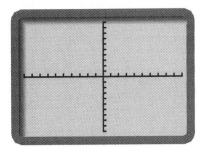

4. Repeat Exercise 3 for the lines in Exercise 2.

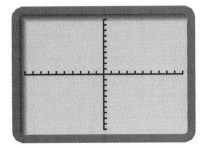

5. Striking designs are produced by combining the graphs in Exercises 1 and 3 and the graphs in Exercises 2 and 4. Under what conditions will the linear function $y = mx + b$ be increasing? When will it be decreasing?

This lesson will help students reach a point where they can picture the graph of a given linear function and encourage them to write coherent sentences.

Exercise 1

In the equation $y = mx + b$, m is the slope of the line, and b is the y-intercept.

Exercise 2

Graph **a**: This function is increasing, so the slope m is positive. Since the line intersects the y-axis above the x-axis, the y-intercept b is positive.

Graph **b**: This function is constant, so the slope m is zero. Since the line intersects the y-axis above the x-axis, the y-intercept b is positive.

Graph **c**: This function is decreasing, so the slope m is negative. Since the line intersects the y-axis above the x-axis, the y-intercept b is positive.

Graph **d**: This function is increasing, so the slope m is positive. Since the line passes through the origin, the y-intercept b is zero.

Graph **e**: This function is constant, so the slope m is zero. Since the line intersects the y-axis below the x-axis, the y-intercept b is negative.

Graph **f**: This function is decreasing, so the slope m is negative. Since the line intersects the y-axis below the x-axis, the y-intercept b is negative.

Graph **g**: This function is decreasing, so the slope m is negative. The line passes through the origin, so the y-intercept b is zero.

Graph **h**: This function is increasing, so the slope m is positive. Since the line intersects the y-axis below the x-axis, the y-intercept b is negative.

LESSON 4.10

You know that all linear functions can be written in the form $y = mx + b$ where y is a function of x.

1. What does m represent? What does b represent? Write complete sentences when you give your answer.

2. For each graph below, tell whether the slope m is positive, negative, or zero. Similarly, tell whether the y-intercept b is positive, negative, or zero. Below each graph, write a sentence giving your answer and explaining your reasoning. For each graph, state whether the function is increasing, decreasing, or constant.

a.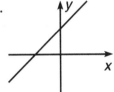

b.

c.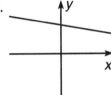

d.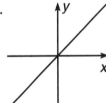

e.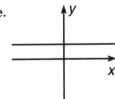

f.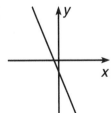

g.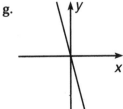

h.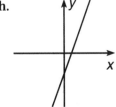

Students have always found the process of translating a word sentence into an algebraic equation difficult. As intermediate exercises, we have provided many examples in which students must find a suitable graph to model a situation. Another approach to help students start modeling is to give multiple-choice exercises like those in this lesson. Although we generally do not associate creativity with the multiple-choice format, you can extend the exercises in a creative fashion by having students look at the incorrect answers and make up situations to fit these equations.

Exercise 1

b; $y = 0.87x$

Exercise 2

c; $y = 20 - 0.87x$

Exercise 3

d; $y = 35 + 6x$

Exercise 4

b; $y = 10x - 50$

Exercise 5

a. Possible answer: 0–10; negative boxes of pasta don't make sense.
b. Check students' tables.
c. For the table entry (10, 8.7), a possible statement is, "The total cost for 10 boxes of pasta is $8.70."

Exercise 6

Sample answers are given.

Exercise 2: For the table entry (1, 19.13), a possible statement is, "If Louis buys 1 box of pasta he will have $19.13 left."

Exercise 3: For the table entry (5, 65), a possible statement is, "If 6 tickets are sold, Maria will have $65 in her cash box."

Exercise 4: For the table entry (17, 120), a possible statement is, "If Carla works 17 hours, her profit will be $120."

1. Pasta costs $0.87 per box. Louis wants to purchase x boxes of pasta. Choose the equation that gives the total cost.
   a. $y = x + 0.87$
   b. $y = 0.87x$
   c. $y = x - 0.87$
   d. $y = 0.87 - x$

2. Louis has $20. Which equation shows how much money he will have left after he purchases x boxes of pasta?
   a. $y = 20 + 0.87x$
   b. $y = 20x - 0.87$
   c. $y = 20 - 0.87x$
   d. $y = 20 - x - 0.87$

3. Maria is selling concert tickets for $6 apiece. If she starts with $35 in her cash box, which equation shows how much money she will have in her cash box after selling x tickets?
   a. $y = 35x + 6$
   b. $y = 35 + x + 6$
   c. $y = 35 - 6x$
   d. $y = 35 + 6x$

4. Carla is starting a business clipping hedges. She charges $10 per hour, but she had to first buy $50 worth of equipment. Choose the equation that shows how much profit she will make.
   a. $y = 50 + 10x$
   b. $y = 10x - 50$
   c. $y = 50 - 10x$
   d. $y = 10 + x - 50$

5. a. Reread Exercise 1. What are some possible values for x that you might want to consider? Explain why you would not be interested in letting $x = -2$.
   b. On your graphing calculator, enter the proper equation. With a TI-82 press the [Y=] key and enter the proper equation as **Y1**. Be sure the other **Y**s are turned off and go to [TblSet]. Now set your table so that the x values from part **a** are in it.
   c. Go to the table and choose any line from it. Use the information given to write a statement in the context of the problem.

6. Repeat Exercise 5 for Exercises 2–4.

In this lesson, students must write their own correct algebraic statements, but the situations closely match ones they have seen on the multiple-choice sheet. All examples are modeled by linear functions. When looking at linear applications, students often forget about slope and intercepts. This poses no problem when lines are studied in the abstract. Students also have trouble taking a point on a line and translating the information it gives into a sentence relating to the situation. The fact that a point is given means that with a graphing calculator students can check their equations using this point. Possible equations and statements are given.

Exercise 1

a. $y = 0.59x$ b. "20 boxes of macaroni will cost $11.80."
c. Slope: 0.59; y-intercept: 0

Exercise 2

a. $y = 0.75x$ b. "22 crunch bars will cost $16.50."
c. Slope: 0.75; y-intercept: 0

Exercise 3

a. $y = 20 - 0.59x$ b. "If I buy 30 boxes of macaroni, I will have $2.30 left."
c. Slope: -0.59; y-intercept: 20

Exercise 4

a. $y = 35 - 0.75x$ b. "If I buy 26 crunch bars, I will have $15.50 left."
c. Slope: -0.75; y-intercept: 35

Exercise 5

a. $y = 2x$ b. "If Pedro sells 45 hot dogs, he will have $90 in his cash box."
c. Slope: 2; y-intercept: 0

Exercise 6

a. $y = 40 + 3x$
b. "If Sue Chin sells 11 tickets, she will have $73 in her cash box."
c. Slope: 3; y-intercept: 40

Exercise 7

a. $y = 21{,}000 + 1500x$
b. "After eleven years of teaching, the teacher's salary will be $37,500."
c. Slope: 1500; y-intercept: 21,000

Exercise 8

a. $y = 5x - 500$ b. "If 355 tickets are sold, the profit will be $1275."
c. Slope: 5; y-intercept: –500

Eight situations are presented. For each one, complete the following:

a. Write an equation for the amount specified.

b. In each situation, the graph of the equation is a line and a point on the line is given. Use that point to write an appropriate statement in terms of the situation.

c. Give the slope and the *y*-intercept of the line.

1. Macaroni costs $0.59 per box. Find the total cost *y* for *x* boxes of macaroni. Point: (20, 11.8)

2. Crunch bars costs $0.75 per bar. Find the total cost *y* for *x* crunch bars. Point: (22, 16.5)

3. You have $20. How much money will you have left after you purchase *x* boxes of macaroni? (Refer to Exercise 1.) Point: (30, 2.3)

4. You have $35. How much money will you have left after you purchase *x* crunch bars? (Refer to Exercise 2.) Point: (26, 15.5)

5. Pedro charges $2 for each hot dog he sells. If he starts with an empty cash box, how much money will be have in his cash box after selling *x* hot dogs? Point: (45, 90)

6. Sue Chin is selling rodeo tickets for $3 apiece. If she starts with $40 in her cash box, how much money will she have in her cash box after selling *x* tickets? Point: (11, 73)

7. A teacher starts her career with a salary of $21,000. Suppose that each year she receives an increase of $1500. What will be her salary *y* after *x* years of teaching? Point: (11, 37,500)

8. The cost for decorations and the band for the homecoming dance is $500. If tickets cost $5 each, what will be the profit if *x* tickets are sold? Point: (355, 1275).

This lesson is designed to help students picture and describe what $y = ax$ looks like for any value of a when compared to $y = x$. It reviews the notion of increasing and decreasing functions and gives situations for which a function of the form $y = ax$ is the appropriate model. Students are also asked to think up such situations on their own.

Exercise 1

Line **a**: $y = \frac{1}{4}x$ Line **b**: $y = \frac{1}{2}x$ Line **c**: $y = x$ Line **d**: $y = 2x$

Line **e**: $y = 3x$ Line **f**: $y = 5x$ Line **g**: $y = -4x$ Line **h**: $y = -\frac{3}{2}x$

Line **i**: $y = -x$ Line **j**: $y = -\frac{2}{3}x$ Line **k**: $y = -\frac{1}{3}x$

You can point out that all of the lines pass through the origin, so the slope is the only unknown. To find the slope, students need only identify a point and find the ratio $\frac{y}{x}$.

Exercise 2

Lines **a**–**f** are increasing; lines **g**–**k** are decreasing.

Exercise 3

All three lines pass through the origin. The line for $y = 45x$ increases more steeply than any line graphed here; the line for $y = -29x$ decreases more steeply than any line; and the line for $y = -\frac{1}{10}x$ decreases less steeply than any line.

Exercise 4

Sample answers are given.

a. If $a > 1$, then $y = ax$ is increasing and increases at a faster rate than $y = x$. The graph of $y = ax$ rises more steeply than the graph of $y = x$.

b. If $0 < a < 1$, then $y = ax$ is increasing, but it increases at a slower rate than $y = x$. The rise of the graph of $y = ax$ is gentler than the rise of the graph of $y = x$.

c. If $a < -1$, then $y = ax$ is decreasing and decreases at a faster rate than $y = -x$. The graph of $y = ax$ falls more steeply than the graph of $y = -x$.

d. If $0 > a > -1$, then $y = ax$ is decreasing but it decreases at a slower rate than $y = -x$. The fall of the line $y = ax$ is gentler than the fall of line $y = -x$.

Exercise 5

Line **b**, $y = \frac{1}{2}x$

Exercise 6

$y = 4.5x$

Exercise 7

$y = 4x$

Exercise 8

Answers will vary.

1. Give an equation for each line graphed on the grid below.

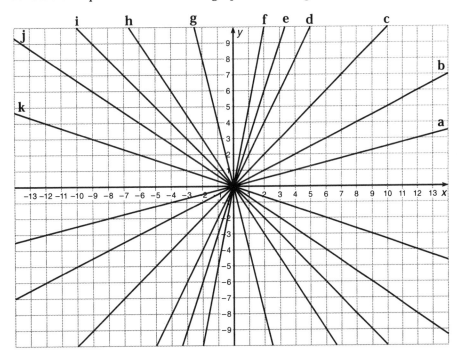

2. Which lines represent increasing functions? Decreasing functions?

3. Describe the graphs of the lines $y = 45x$, $y = -29x$, and $y = -\frac{1}{10}x$. Where would they appear on the grid?

4. Compare the graph of $y = ax$ with the graph of $y = x$ when a is positive and with the graph of $y = -x$ when a is negative. Complete each sentence.
   a. If $a > 1$, then _____.
   b. If $1 > a > 0$, then _____.
   c. If $a < -1$, then _____.
   d. If $-1 < a < 0$, then _____.

5. A man sells pretzels for $0.50 each. Which of the graphs in Exercise 1 would be useful for determining the amount of money he makes for selling any number of pretzels?

6. Clerks at a fast-food restaurant are paid $4.50 per hour. Give the function that will indicate a clerk's wages for any number of hours.

7. What is the relationship between the perimeter of a square and the length of a side? Give the function that will indicate the perimeter of a square for any side length.

8. Make up a problem in which you need to use a *linear* function to find a total as in Exercises 5 and 6 above.

Many of the remaining lessons in this chapter are most easily done with graphing calculators. They are designed to help the student to see that a function can be represented by a graph, a table of values, or an algebraic equation. With each representation, the student uses a piece of information to make a relevant statement about the original situation. Each lesson also includes the standard type of question that teachers ask when dealing with a linear equation, that is, "Given x, what is y?" or "Given y, what is x?" We ask the student to explain how to do such problems both algebraically and graphically. Finally, we ask the student to think about how a change in algebraic properties (namely the slope and y-intercept) affects the verbal situation that gave rise to the linear function in the first place.

Exercise 1

Sample equation: $y = 8.50 + 0.35x$; function notation: $W(x) = 8.50 + 0.35x$

Exercise 2

x: number of units produced per hour; y: wage earned per hour

Exercise 3

For the point (30, 19), a possible statement is, "If a worker produces 30 units per hour, he should be paid $19 per hour." Check students' second statements; a negative number of units doesn't make sense.

Exercise 4

Sample answers: $0 < x < 50$ and $0 < y < 50$; 5 units per grid line on both axes

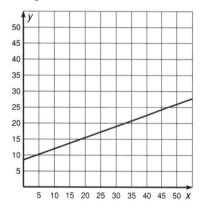

Exercise 5

Sample table:

x	y
10	12
20	15.5
40	22.5
50	26

For the point (40, 22.5), a possible statement is, "If a worker produces 40 units per hour, he should be paid $22.50 per hour."

Exercise 6

$13.05; to solve algebraically, substitute 13 for x in the equation and find y; to solve with a graphing calculator, use the $\boxed{\text{TRACE}}$ feature to find the point with x-coordinate 13, or use the tables.

Exercise 7

42 units; to solve algebraically, substitute 23.2 for y in the equation and solve for x; to solve with a graphing calculator, use the $\boxed{\text{TRACE}}$ feature to find the point with y-coordinate 23.2, or use the tables.

Exercise 8

Slope: 0.35; y-intercept: 8.5; if the y-intercept is increased by 1, the fixed hourly rate is increased by $1; if the slope is increased by 0.2, the piecework rate is increased by $0.20. If the worker produces 5 units or more per hour, he would opt to increase the slope by 0.2; if the worker produces fewer than 5 units per hour, he would want to increase the y-intercept by 1.

Graph

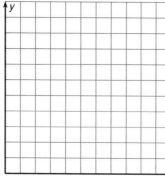

Algebraic Representation

All ordered pairs (x, y) such that

$y =$ _____

$W(x) =$ _____

Table

x	y

A manufacturer pays his assembly line workers $8.50 per hour. In addition, workers receive a piecework rate of $0.35 per unit produced.

1. In the space above, complete the equation $y = ...$, which gives hourly wages as a function of the number of units produced per hour. Then complete the function $w(x) = ...$.

2. Enter your equation in your calculator and graph it. What does x represent? What does y represent?

3. (30, 19) is a point on the line. Write a statement that gives information the manufacturer can use. Find another point on the line, and write another statement for the manufacturer. Explain why you should choose a point for which the x-coordinate is a positive integer.

4. On the grid above, sketch the graph of your function. What is a good choice for the range of x if it is impossible to produce more than 50 units per hour? What is a good choice for the range of y? Justify your choices. Give your scales.

5. A function can also be represented by a table of values. Fill in several lines of the table above, choosing appropriate x values and calculating the corresponding y values. Pick a line in the table and use the information given in the line to write a statement about a worker.

6. How much would a worker earn if he produced 13 units? Tell how to solve this problem both algebraically and graphically using your graphing calculator.

7. If a worker earned $23.20 for 1 hour, how many units did he produce? Tell how to solve this problem both algebraically and graphically.

8. The function you have graphed is linear. Give the slope of the line and the y-intercept of the line. If a worker had the choice to increase the slope by 0.2 or the y-intercept by 1, which should he choose to do? Justify your answer with an explanation. Explain the effect of each change on his salary.

LESSON 4.15 TEACHER NOTES

Exercise 1

Sample equation: $y = 19.50 + 0.2x$; function notation: $R(x) = 19.50 + 0.2x$

Exercise 2

x: number of miles traveled per day; *y:* rental charge for the day

Exercise 3

For the point (40, 27.5), a possible statement is, "If George drives 40 miles in a day, he will be charged $27.50 for renting a car." Check students' second statements; a negative number of miles traveled doesn't make sense.

Exercise 4

Sample answers: $0 < x < 1000$ and $0 < y < 250$; 100 units per grid line on the *x*-axis and 50 units per grid line on the *y*-axis

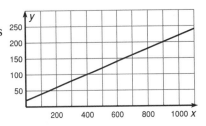

Exercise 5

Sample table:

x	y
100	39.5
200	59.5
300	79.5
400	99.5

For the point (200, 59.5), a possible statement is, "If Mary drives 200 miles in a day, she will be charged $59.50 for renting a car."

Exercise 6

$74.50; to solve algebraically, substitute 275 for *x* in the equation and find *y;* to solve with a graphing calculator, use the TRACE feature to find the point with *x*-coordinate 275, or use the tables.

Exercise 7

365 miles; to solve algebraically, substitute 92.5 for *y* in the equation and solve for *x;* to solve with a graphing calculator, use the TRACE feature to find the point with *y*-coordinate 92.5, or use the tables.

Exercise 8

Slope: 0.2; *y*-intercept: 19.5; if the rental charge is $25 per day and $0.15 per mile, the *y*-intercept is 25 and the slope is 0.15. Sample answer: the second rental agency; for 250 miles, the rental charge is less.

Graph

Algebraic Representation

All ordered pairs (x, y) such that

$y =$ _____

$R(x) =$ _____

Table

x	y

A rental agency rents cars at $19.50 per day plus $0.20 per mile.

1. In the space above, complete the equation $y = ...$, which gives the rental charge after 1 day as a function of the number of miles driven. Then complete the function $R(x) = ...$

2. Enter your equation in your calculator and graph it. What does x represent? What does y represent?

3. (40, 27.5) is a point on the line. Write a statement that gives information that the renter of the car can use. Find another point on the line, and write another statement for the renter. Explain why you should choose a point for which the x-coordinate is a positive integer.

4. On the grid above, sketch the graph of your function. What is a good choice for the range of x? Think of how far you can drive in a day. What is a good choice for the range of y? Justify your choices. Give your scales.

5. A function can also be represented by a table of values. Fill in several lines of the table above, choosing appropriate x values and calculating the corresponding y values. Pick a line in the table and use the information given in the line to write a statement about a car rental.

6. How much money would a man owe if he drove 275 miles? Tell how to solve this problem both algebraically and graphically using your graphing calculator.

7. Suppose a rental costs $92.50 for the day. How far was the car driven? Again, tell how to solve this problem both algebraically and graphically.

8. The function you have graphed is linear. Give the slope of the line and the y-intercept of the line. If a rental agency charges $25 per day and $0.15 per mile and you planned to drive 250 miles that day, which agency would you choose? Justify your answer with an explanation.

LESSON 4.16 TEACHER NOTES

Exercise 1

Sample equation: $y = 0.65x$; function notation: $S(x) = 0.65x$

Exercise 2

x: original price; *y:* sale price

Exercise 3

For the point (51, 33.15), a possible statement is, "If the original price of an item is $51, the sale price is $33.15." Check students' second statements; a negative price doesn't make sense.

Exercise 4

Sample answers: $0 < x < 1000$ and $0 < y < 650$; 100 units per grid line on the *x*-axis and 50 units per grid line on the *y*-axis

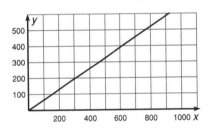

Exercise 5

Sample table:

x	y
40	26
60	39
80	52
100	65

For the point (80, 52), a possible statement is, "If the original price of an item is $80, the sale price will be $52."

Exercise 6

$243.75; to solve algebraically, substitute 375 for *x* in the equation and find *y*; to solve with a graphing calculator, use the TRACE feature to find the point with *x*-coordinate 375, or use the tables.

Exercise 7

$200; to solve algebraically, substitute 130 for *y* in the equation and solve for *x*; to solve with a graphing calculator, use the TRACE feature to find the point with *y*-coordinate 130, or use the tables.

Exercise 8

Sample answer: As a customer, I would want to decrease the slope by 0.05 because this would result in a sale price 40% off the original price.

Graph

y

x

Algebraic Representation

All ordered pairs (x, y) such that

$y =$ _____

$S(x) =$ _____

Table

x	y

A clothing store is having 35%-off sale on all items.

1. In the space above, complete the equation $y = ...$, which gives the sale price as function of the original price. Then complete the function $S(x) = ...$

2. Enter your equation in your calculator and graph it. What does x represent? What does y represent?

3. (51, 33.15) is a point on the line. Write a statement that gives information about the sale. Find another point on the line, and write another statement about the sale.

4. On the grid above, sketch the graph of your function. What is a good choice for the range of x, considering the store is a clothing store? What is a good choice for the range of y? Justify your choices. Give your scales.

5. A function can also be represented by a table of values. Fill in several lines of the table above, choosing appropriate x values and calculating the corresponding y values. Pick a line in the table and use the information given in the line to write a statement about the sale.

6. If the original price is $375, what is the sale price? Tell how to do this problem both algebraically and graphically using your graphing calculator.

7. If the sale price of an item is $130, what was the original price? Again, tell how to solve this problem both algebraically and graphically.

8. Suppose you are a customer and you are given the opportunity to increase or decrease the slope of the line by 0.05. Which should you choose to do? What is the effect of your choice on the sale? Justify your answer with an explanation.

Problems involving cost, revenue, and profit occur frequently. As students often have difficulty differentiating between costs and revenue, emphasize that costs are money paid out and revenue is money taken in.

Exercise 1

Revenue equation: $y = 12x$;
cost equation: $y = 0.5x + 485$;
profit equation: $y = 11.5x - 485$

Exercise 2

For all three equations, x represents the number of yards mowed and y represents an amount of money in dollars.

A possible statement for the revenue equation is: "(11, 132) is a point on the revenue line. If you mow 11 yards, your revenue will be $132."

A possible statement for the cost equation is: "(10, 490) is a point on the cost line. After mowing 10 yards, your total cost for the summer will be $490."

A possible statement for the profit equation is: "(100, 665) is a point on the profit line. After mowing 100 yards, your total profit for the summer will be $665."

Exercise 3

The profit and revenue lines appear to be parallel because their slopes are nearly the same. However, they are not parallel because one has a slope of 12 and the other line a slope of 11.5.

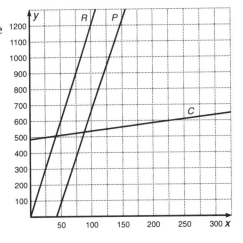

Exercise 4

43 yards

Exercise 5

Answers will vary. Four per day would mean 28 per week, for a weekly revenue of $336.

Exercise 6

At least 130 yards

Exercise 7

As the years go by, your fixed cost might be only a service maintenance charge for your mower, and your profits will go up.

Suppose you are setting up a lawn-mowing business for summer vacation. You buy a power mower for $485. The cost of gasoline to mow a lawn averages $0.50. You charge $12 per yard.

1. The amount you make before subtracting your costs is called *revenue*. Revenue is what you bring in; costs are what you pay out. Write a revenue equation and a cost equation. Form a profit equation by subtracting cost from revenue.

2. Graph the three equations. What does *x* represent? What does *y* represent? Find an appropriate point on each line and use the information to write a statement about your business using the information given by each point.

3. Sketch graphs of the three equations on the grid below. Be careful to choose a scale that will accommodate all three lines. Explain why two of the lines appear parallel but are not.

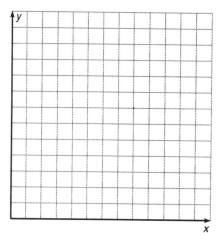

4. How many yards will you need to mow in order to break even?

5. How many yards do you think you could realistically mow in one week? What would be your weekly revenue at that rate?

6. If you need to make $1000 profit in order to go on a trip, how many yards must you mow?

7. Why might you plan to stay in business for several summers rather than just for one summer?

Exercise 1

The line through (0, 0) is the revenue line, as when nothing is produced, no money comes in. The line with positive y-intercept is the cost line, with the y-intercept giving us the amount of the fixed costs. The third line is the profit line, which is the difference of the revenue and the costs.

Exercise 2

The costs line; it indicates that the fixed costs of the business are $126.

Exercise 3

The profit line; it indicates that the business will break even if 176 items are produced and sold.

Exercise 4

The profits will continue to increase as the distance between the revenue and cost lines increases.

Suppose you plan to start a small manufacturing business. You will have certain fixed one-time costs and then a specific unit cost for each item produced. The fixed amount you charge per item will be your revenue. Your profit will be the difference between your revenue and your costs. Below is a graph with three lines, one representing your costs, one representing revenue, and one representing profit.

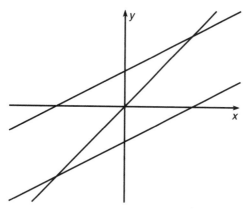

1. Identify which line represents costs, which one revenue, and which one profit. Explain your reasoning.

2. Suppose (0, 126) is a point on one of the lines. Tell which line contains this point. What information does this point give regarding your business venture?

3. Suppose (176, 0) is a point on one of the lines. Tell which line contains this point. What information does this point give regarding your business venture?

4. In this model, does your profit continue to increase as you produce more? Explain your answer.

Exercise 1

The line through (0, 0) is the revenue line, as when nothing is produced, no money comes in. The line with positive y-intercept is the cost line, with the y-intercept giving us the amount of the fixed costs. The third line is the profit line, which is the difference of the revenue and the costs.

Exercise 2

(0, 375)

Exercise 3

The point of intersection of the cost and revenue lines, (500, 1250)

Exercise 4

Sample equations are given.

Cost line: $y = 1.75x + 375$. The two points (0, 375) and (500, 1250) give a slope of 1.75, while the y-intercept is 375.

Revenue line: $y = 2.5x$. The two points (0, 0) and (500, 1250) give a slope of 2.5, while the y-intercept is 0.

Profit line: $y = 0.75x - 375$ is found by subtracting costs from revenue.

Suppose you plan to start a small manufacturing business. You will have certain fixed one-time costs and then a specific unit cost for each item produced. The fixed amount you charge per item will be your revenue. Your profit will be the difference between your revenue and your costs. Below is a graph with three lines, one representing your costs, one representing revenue, and one representing profit.

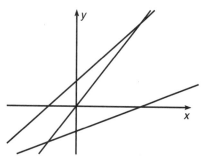

1. Identify which line represents costs, which one revenue, and which one profit. Explain your reasoning.

2. Suppose your fixed costs are $375. This information gives the coordinates of a certain point on the graph. What is that point?

3. Suppose that the production and sale of 500 items result in a revenue of $1250 and costs of $1250. This information gives you the coordinates of another on the graph. What is that point?

4. Use the points you found in Exercises 2 and 3 to write equations for costs, revenue, and profit.

Because of the large numbers, it is suggested that students do not try to complete this lesson without graphing calculators.

Exercise 1

Sample equation: $y = -1687.5x + 18,000$, found by using the two points (0, 18,000) and (8, 4500) to determine the slope -1687.5; in function notation,
$V(x) = -1687.5x + 18,000$

Exercise 2

x: number of years since purchase; *y:* value of the truck; the slope is the decrease in value per year.

Exercise 3

For the point (3.25, 12,515.625), a possible statement is, "After 3 years 3 months, the truck will be worth about $12,516."

Exercise 4

Sample answers: $0 < x < 10$ and $0 < y < 20,000$; 1 unit per grid line on *x*-axis and 2000 units per grid line on *y*-axis

Exercise 5

Table and graph from a graphing calculator are given.

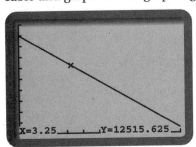

X	Y1
0	18000
1	16313
2	14625
3	12938
4	11250
5	9562.5
6	7875

X=0

X=3.25   Y=12515.625

Exercise 6

$8718.75; to solve algebraically, substitute 5.5 for *x* in the equation and find *y;* to solve with a graphing calculator, use the [TRACE] feature to find the point with *x*-coordinate 5.5, or use the tables.

Exercise 7

$7\frac{1}{9}$ years; to solve algebraically, substitute 6000 for *y* in the equation and solve for *x*; to solve with a graphing calculator, use the [TRACE] feature to find the point with *y*-coordinate 6000, or use the tables.

Exercise 8

Sample answer: as the owner of the truck, I would prefer that the slope would increase, as the truck would be worth more for a longer period of time. I would prefer the *y*-intercept to decrease, so the original price would be lower.

Graph

Algebraic Representation

All ordered pairs (*x, y*) such that

y = _____

V(*x*) = _____

Table

x	*y*

A man buys a truck for $18,000. Eight years later, it has a salvage value of $4,500.

1. Assume that the truck's depreciation is linear. In the space above, complete the equation *y* = ..., which gives the value of the truck as a function of time from the date of purchase. Then complete the function *V*(*x*) = ...

2. Enter your equation in your calculator and graph it. What does *x* represent? What does *y* represent? What does the slope of the line represent?

3. (3.25, 12,515.625) is a point on the line. Use this information to write a statement about the value of the truck.

4. On the grid above, sketch the graph of your function. What is a good choice for the range of *x*? What is a good choice for the range of *y*? Justify your choices. Indicate your scales.

5. A function can also be represented by a table of values. Fill in several lines of the table above, choosing appropriate *x* values and calculating the corresponding *y* values. Pick a line in the table and use the information given in the line to write a statement about the truck.

6. How much is the truck worth after 5 years 6 months? Tell how to do this problem both algebraically and graphically using your graphing calculator.

7. When was the truck worth $6000? Again, tell how to solve this problem both algebraically and graphically.

8. As the owner of the truck, would you prefer the slope of this line to increase or decrease? Would you prefer the *y*-intercept to increase or decrease? Justify your answer with an explanation.

In Lesson 21, three situations are given. Students must identify which graph, which table, and which equation match each situation. Choosing a correct graph is similar to the exercises in Chapter 1. You may suggest students use the graph to help them choose the correct table. The graph should also indicate what type of equation is appropriate for each situation. Then students are asked to describe in words what happens to the y values in the correct table as the x values increase from 0 to 5. Tell students to comment on increase and decrease and on rate of increase and decrease. The lesson is designed to help students understand that a function can be described by a table of values as well as by a graph and an equation.

Exercise 1

Graph **d**, table **Y2**, equation **a**; a possible statement is, "As x increases from 0 to 5, y increases steadily from 0 to 130 by 26 units for each unit increase in x."

Exercise 2

Graph **a**, table **Y1**, equation **b**; a possible statement is, "As x increases from 0 to 5, y first increases from 0 to 100 and then decreases back to 0."

Exercise 3

Graph **c**, table **Y3**, equation **d**; a possible statement is, "As x increases from 0 to 5, y increases from 0 to nearly 100. The increase is rapid at first and then slows down."

For each of the three situations, choose a graph, a table (Y1, Y2, or Y3), and an equation from those given that best describes the desired function. Then write a sentence describing how the *y* values change as the *x* values increase from 0 to 5 in the table you chose.

1. A painter charges $26 per hour. Represent the painter's earnings as a function of time.

2. A firecracker was fired into the air. Represent the height of the firecracker as a function of time.

3. Chris had to learn the names of 100 plant species during the semester. At first he learned quickly, but then his learning rate decreased. Represent the number of words Chris learned as a function of time.

Graphs

a.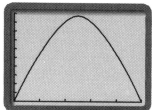
b.

c.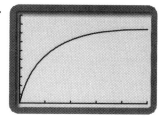
d.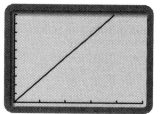

Tables

X	Y₁	Y₂	Y₃
0	0	0	0
.5	36	13	36.754
1	64	26	60
1.5	84	39	74.702
2	96	52	84
2.5	100	65	89.881
3	96	78	93.6
3.5	84	91	95.952
4	64	104	97.44
4.5	36	117	98.381
5	0	130	98.976

Equations

a. $y = 26x$ **b.** $y = -16x^2 + 80x$ **c.** $x = 5$ **d.** $y = 100(1 - 0.4^x)$

Note: You may graph these equations on a graphing calculator. Use the tables to help you set the windows.

LESSON 4.22 TEACHER NOTES

The exercises in Lessons 4.22 and 4.23 refer to applications commonly looked at in current algebra texts. They are designed to make the student think about a graph in its entirety. These lessons are similar to many of the lessons in Chapter 1 and are included here because students in an algebra course often lose sight of the fact that they should have definite expectations regarding the appearance of the graph of a certain situation. Have students explain their choices and why the other graphs are not appropriate.

Exercise 1

Graph **c**

Exercise 2

Graph **b**; a common mistake is to choose graph **a** because the sentence evokes a mental picture of the submarine's movement, so ask the students to think about what happens to depth as the submarine descends.

Exercise 3

Graph **d**

Exercise 4

Graph **b**; many students may choose graph **a**, so point out that no matter how much water is added, there will still be some acid present.

For each set of graphs, choose the one that best matches the situation.

1. A baseball is hit. Its height *h* is a function of time *t*.

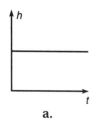
a.

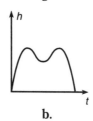
b.

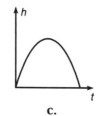
c.

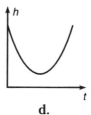
d.

2. A submarine submerges, rises up to the surface, and submerges again. Its depth *d* is a funtion of time *t*.

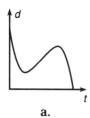
a.

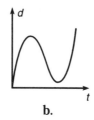
b.

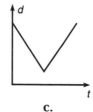
c.

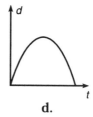
d.

3. The more miles you drive in a rented car, the more you have to pay the rental agency. The amount owed *A* is a function of miles *m* traveled.

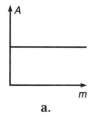
a.

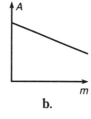
b.

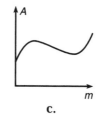
c.

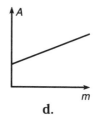
d.

4. As water is added to the solution, the percent of acid present decreases. The percent of acid present *a* is a function of amount of water added *w*. Write a sentence explaining why you made the particular choice you did.

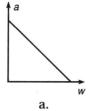
a.

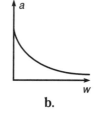
b.

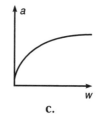
c.

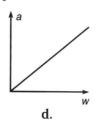
d.

Exercise 1

Graph **d**; as time passes, Emily goes up and down repeatedly on the Ferris wheel.

Exercise 2

Graph **e** or **h**; both imply there is a price no one is willing to pay. On the other hand, **e** indicates that there is only a certain number of people interested in the product even if it is given away free. Students might not agree with the last statement and may feel that graph **h** is the correct answer. Economists often graph price as a function of demand.

Exercise 3

Graph **h**; in this case, graph **e** is not correct, as things cool exponentially.

Exercise 4

Graph **a**; Fred is paid a steady hourly wage, so the graph is linear.

Exercise 5

Graph **b**; the firecracker goes up and then comes back down.

Exercise 6

Graph **g**; it is the only graph in which the rate of increase is increasing.

Exercise 7

Graph **c**; it is the graph of a constant function.

Exercise 8

Graph **f**; it shows a rise, a fall, and then another rise.

Read each sentence and decide which of the graphs below matches the situation.

1. As Emily rides round and round on a Ferris wheel, her height off the ground is a function of time.

2. As the price goes up, the demand for the product goes down. Price is a function of demand. Assume there may be a price so high no one would pay it.

3. A cup of hot coffee cools to room temperature. Temperature is a function of time.

4. The more Fred works, the more money he earns. Wages are a function of hours worked.

5. A firecracker is fired into the air. Height is a function of time.

6. Bacteria increased at an increasing rate. The number of bacteria is a function of time.

7. The temperature held steady at 80° F. Temperature is a function of time.

8. The temperature rose, then fell, and then rose again. Temperature is a function of time.

a.   b.   c.   d.

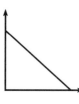  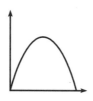  

e.   f.   g.   h.

This exercise is good for algebra students when they are formally being introduced to exponential functions. It gives them a good sense of what exponential functions of the form $y = ab^{kx}$ will look like.

Exercise 1

Graph **b**; students should see that growth at an increasing rate is pictured by a curve that is concave up, rather than by a straight line or a curve that is concave down. Students must then consider scale to choose which of graphs **b** and **d** is correct.

Exercise 2

Graph **a**; students should see that decrease at a decreasing rate is again pictured by a curve that is concave up and not by a straight line or a curve that is concave down.

Exercise 3

a. Ridge Top High; the constant is -32.
b. At a slower rate from year to year
c. Graph A
d. Ridge Top High: graph A, the straight line; Mountain Valley High: graph B, the curved line

For each set of graphs in Exercises 1 and 2, choose the one that best matches the situation.

1. If you invest $500 at 6% annual interest, your money grows at a faster rate each year. After 50 years you will have $9210.

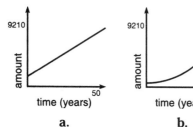 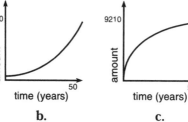 

      a.   **b.**   **c.**   **d.**

2. If a school's enrollment decreases by 3% annually, the enrollment declines at a slower and slower rate. If the enrollment is 1875 now, it will be close to 400 students 50 years from now.

 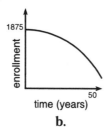  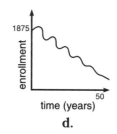

      a.   **b.**   **c.**   **d.**

3. At Ridge Top High School, the enrollment is decreasing by 32 students each year. In Mountain Valley School, the enrollment is decreasing by 3% annually. Both schools start with 2000 students. The graph below shows how the enrollments change at the two schools.

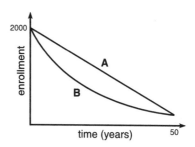

  a. For which school is the annual rate of change constant?

  b. Does Mountain Valley enrollment decrease at the same, a slower, or a faster rate from year to year?

  c. Which graph has a constant slope?

  d. Which graph shows the enrollment of Ridge Top High, and which shows the enrollment of Mountain Valley High?

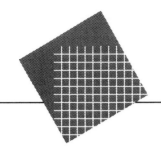

GLOSSARY

These definitions are not formal definitions. They are only an aid to reading the text.

absolute value The distance a number is from zero on a number line

acceleration The rate of change in the speed of a moving body

algebra A mathematical language used to model real-world problems; the study of variables and arithmetic operations using variables

asymptote A line approached by the graph of a function

axis, axes The perpendicular number lines in a coordinate system from which coordinates of points are determined

coefficient A number multiplied by a variable or variables

complement of an angle Either of two angles, the sum of whose measures is 90°

concave Curving in, cupped

concave down Curving in and opening downward

concave up Curving in and opening upward

congruent Having the same size and shape

constant Unchanging

constant function A function whose y values remain the same for all values of x

coordinate plane The plane formed by two perpendicular, intersecting number lines

coordinates An ordered pair of numbers used to locate a point in the coordinate plane

cubic function A polynomial function of the third degree; a function whose equation is in the form $y = ax^3 + bx^2 + cx + d$ where $a \neq 0$

decay Disintegration over time

decreasing function A function whose y values decrease as its x values increase

density The quantity of matter in a unit of volume or area

dependent variable A variable whose value depends upon the value(s) of another variable(s)

depreciation The decrease in value over time

direct variation The relationship between two variables x and y such that $y = kx$ for some constant k

Distance Formula A formula for the distance between points (x_1, y_1) and (x_2, y_2): $\sqrt{(y_2 - y_1)^2 + (x_2 - x_1)^2}$

domain The set of values that may be substituted for an independent variable; the set of x values in a relation

endpoint The point at the end of a segment or ray

equation A sentence with an equal sign

exponential function A function in the form $y = ca^{kx} + b$

expression A mathematical phrase that uses numbers and/or variables and operation symbols to represent a value

force The cause that produces, changes, or stops the motion of a body

frustum The portion of a pyramid or a cone that lies between the base and a parallel cross-section of the figure

function A relation between two quantities (one commonly labeled input or x, the other output or y) that yields exactly one output value for each input value; a set of ordered pairs in which each first coordinate (input value) appears with exactly one second coordinate (output value)

function notation Notation to indicate a function, such as $f(x)$, read "f of x"

gravity The force of attraction that makes objects move or tend to move toward each other

grid Arrangement of vertical and horizonal lines

horizontal axis The x-axis in a coordinate plane

hypotenuse The side opposite the right angle in a right triangle

increasing function A function whose y values increase as its x values increase

independent variable A variable upon whose value other variables depend

indirect variation The relationship between two variables x and y such that $y = \dfrac{k}{x}$, for some constant k

infinity A quantity without limits

initial velocity Beginning speed

intercept The point where a line crosses the x-axis or the y-axis

interval A section of the real number line

linear Like a straight line

linear function A function with an equation of the form $y = mx + b$

line segment The set of points including two endpoints and all points between them

mass The measure of the quantity of matter a body contains

maximum value The greatest value in a set of numbers; the y-coordinate of the highest point in a graph

minimum value The least value in a set of numbers; the y-coordinate of the lowest point in a graph

negative slope Slope that results if y decreases as x increases

opposite A number whose sum with another number is zero

origin The point $(0, 0)$ on a coordinate grid

parabola A curve whose equation is of the form $y = ax^2 + bx + c$, where $a \neq 0$

perpendicular Meeting at right, or $90°$, angles

piecewise function A function defined with different equations for different parts of the domain

point of intersection The point at which two things meet

positive slope Slope that results if y increases as x increases

profit The gain from a business; income less costs

Pythagorean theorem The formula $a^2 + b^2 = c^2$, where a and b are the lengths of sides in a right triangle and c is the length of the hypotenuse

quadrant One of the four regions determined by the x- and y-axes on the coordinate plane

quadratic function A function with equation $y = ax^2 + bx + c$, where $a \neq 0$

range The set of values of a dependent variable; in a relation, the set of y values

rate The quotient of two quantities with different units

rate of change A number that indicates how one quantity is changing with respect to another

ratio The quotient of two numbers

reciprocal A number whose product with another number is 1

regression equation An equation for a curve of best fit for a set of data points

relation A set of ordered pairs

revenue Income

scale Units of measure along the axes in a coordinate plane

scatterplot A coordinate graph of individual points

slope A number that measures the steepness of a line; the rate of change between points on a line; for two points (x_1, y_1) and (x_2, y_2) the ratio $\frac{y_2 - y_1}{x_2 - x_1}$

straight angle An angle whose measure is 180°

tick mark A mark used to indicate intervals along a number line or axis

upper bounds Upper limits

velocity Speed with direction indicated

vertical axis The y-axis in a coordinate plane

volume The measure of space inside a three-dimensional figure

x-coordinate The first coordinate of an ordered pair

x-intercept The x-coordinate of the point where a graph crosses the x-axis

xy-plane A coordinate plane formed by x- and y-axes

y-coordinate The second coordinate of an ordered pair

y-intercept The y-coordinate of the point where a graph crosses the y-axis